Flare Path

A Play

Terence Rattigan

A Samuel French Acting Edition

SAMUEL FRENCH

FOUNDED 1830

SAMUELFRENCH.COM
SAMUELFRENCH-LONDON.CO.UK

FOR PRODUCTION ENQUIRIES

UNITED STATES AND CANADA
Info@SamuelFrench.com
1-866-598-8449

UNITED KINGDOM AND EUROPE
Theatre@SamuelFrench-London.co.uk
020-7255-4302

Each title is subject to availability from Samuel French, depending upon country of performance. Please be aware that *FLARE PATH* may not be licensed by Samuel French in your territory. Professional and amateur producers should contact the nearest Samuel French office or licensing partner to verify availability.

FLARE PATH

Produced on August 13th, 1942, at the Apollo Theatre, London, with the following cast of characters :

(In order of their appearance)

COUNTESS SKRICZEVINSKY	*Adrianne Allen.*
PETER KYLE	*Martin Walker.*
MRS. OAKES	*Dora Gregory.*
SERGEANT MILLER	*Leslie Dwyer.*
PERCY	*George Cole.*
COUNT SKRICZEVINSKY	*Gerard Hinze.*
FLIGHT-LIEUTENANT GRAHAM . . .	*Jack Watling.*
PATRICIA GRAHAM	*Phyllis Calvert.*
	(By courtesy of Gainsborough Pictures (1928) Ltd.)
MRS. MILLER	*Kathleen Harrison.*
SQUADRON-LEADER SWANSON . . .	*Ivan Samson.*
CORPORAL JONES	*John Bradley.*

Directed by ANTHONY ASQUITH.

Setting by RUTH KEATING.

SYNOPSIS OF SCENES

ACT I

The residents' lounge of the Falcon Hotel at Milchester, Lincs. About 6 p.m. Saturday.

ACT II

SCENE 1.—The same. About three hours later.

SCENE 2.—The same. About 5.30 the following morning.

ACT III

The same. About 12 noon the same day (Sunday).

MUSIC USE NOTE

Licensees are solely responsible for obtaining formal written permission from copyright owners to use copyrighted music in the performance of this play and are strongly cautioned to do so. If no such permission is obtained by the licensee, then the licensee must use only original music that the licensee owns and controls. Licensees are solely responsible and liable for all music clearances and shall indemnify the copyright owners of the play(s) and their licensing agent, Samuel French, against any costs, expenses, losses and liabilities arising from the use of music by licensees. Please contact the appropriate music licensing authority in your territory for the rights to any incidental music.

IMPORTANT BILLING AND CREDIT REQUIREMENTS

If you have obtained performance rights to this title, please refer to your licensing agreement for important billing and credit requirements.

FLARE PATH

ACT I

SCENE.—*The residents' lounge of the Falcon Hotel at Milchester, Lincs.*

Down R. *is a door marked Lounge Bar. Up* R. *is a curved counter marked " Reception," behind which is a door bearing the label " Private." Back* R. *is a door leading on to the road. There are large bow windows at back, with window seats, and a staircase* L., *leading to a small landing at back and thence curving out of sight. Up* L. *is a door marked Coffee Room. Centre* L. *is a fireplace, with fire burning.*

On the rise of the CURTAIN *the sole occupant of the room is* DORIS SKRICZEVINSKY, *a carelessly dressed woman in the early thirties inclined to fat. She has fallen asleep in a large armchair, below the fireplace, a copy of " Everybody's " open on her lap.*

(Effects Cues : No. 1, B.B.C. music ; No. 2, Car door slam ; No. 3, Car driving away.)

A wireless at her side is playing music. A car door is heard slamming and a car drives away. PETER KYLE, *a man of about thirty-five, dressed in correct country attire—too correct to be convincing—comes in from the road, carrying a suitcase. He looks round, then goes up to the reception desk, puts down his suitcase, hat and coat on the chair up* R., *and rings a small handbell. Nothing happens. He rings again.* DORIS *wakes up.*

DORIS *(calling)*. Mrs. Oakes !

*(*MRS. OAKES *comes in from the door marked " Private " (her office). She is a tall, angular woman of middle age.)*

(The music fades on the wireless.)

MRS. OAKES. Yes ? *(Seeing* PETER.*)* Yes ? What can I do for you ?
PETER. I'd like a room, please.
MRS. OAKES. Single or double ?
PETER. Single.
MRS. OAKES. Quite impossible. I'm sorry.

(A slight pause. Then :)

(Effects Cue No 4 : B.B.C. Announcer.)

ANNOUNCER. Hullo, Forces ! " Round the World in Eighty Days." A dramatization of the novel——

5

(DORIS *switches it off.* MRS. OAKES, *paying no further attention to* PETER, *has come from behind her counter to collect a tea-tray off the fender.*)

DORIS (*derisively*). Round the world in eighty days ! They do think up some queer ones, I must say.

MRS. OAKES. I never listen these days, except to the news. Finished with your tea, Countess ?

DORIS. Yes, thank you, Mrs. Oakes.

(MRS. OAKES *takes up the tray and crosses* R. PETER *is watching her, exasperated.*)

MRS. OAKES. Of course, I'm not saying it would be easy to think up new things all the time——

PETER (*loudly*). What about a double ?

MRS. OAKES. You said you wanted a single.

PETER. Yes, but if you haven't got a single, I'd like a double.

MRS. OAKES. I'm sorry. We're full right up. (*She goes behind the counter and closes the flap.*)

PETER. Then why did you give me the choice of asking for a single or a double ?

MRS. OAKES. You might have been a married couple.

PETER. I might have been a sultan and full harem, but I don't see that makes any difference. If you haven't got a room you haven't got a room, have you ?

MRS. OAKES (*unmoved*). No. We haven't got a room.

(*She goes into her office, carrying the tea-tray.* PETER *turns round.*)

PETER. God, what a——

DORIS (*rises and comes* C. *slightly. Excitedly*). Why, it is !

PETER. I beg your pardon.

DORIS. You're Peter Kyle, aren't you ?

PETER. Yes, I am. (*Down to her,* C. *Politely.*) I'm afraid——

DORIS. Oh no. You wouldn't know me. I saw " Light of Love " in Milchester only yesterday. Isn't that funny ?

PETER (*abstractedly*). Yes, it is. (*He makes an obvious effort to be polite.*) It's over two years old—" Light of Love."

DORIS. Oh, we only get the old ones in Milchester. Well, I never—this is a thrill !

PETER. It wasn't a good picture either, I'm afraid.

DORIS. Oh, it was quite good, really. One or two bits were rather silly, I thought. You were ever so good, though.

PETER. Thank you very much.

DORIS. Not at all. I always think you're good.

(*She stares at him in wonder and awe.* PETER *is evidently not unaccustomed to this. He extends his hand, graciously.*)

PETER. How do you do ?

DORIS. Oh, how do you do ? My name's Doris. I won't tell you the other name because you'd never be able to pronounce it. You came over here to arrange about your new picture, didn't you ? I read all about it in the " Express." And how you're giving all your salary to the Red Cross. I do think that's fine. Of course, you are English, aren't you ?

PETER. By birth, yes. But I've been an American citizen for the last seven years.

DORIS. Well, well, well. Peter Kyle ! Would you believe it—drifting into the old Falcon—just like that—and asking for a room.

PETER. And not getting it.

DORIS (*crosses behind the sofa to the counter*). Oh, don't you worry about that. The idea ! (*Calling.*) Mrs. Oakes !

(MRS. OAKES *emerges from her office.*)

MRS. OAKES. Yes ? (*Glaring at* PETER.) I thought I told you——

DORIS (*excitedly*). Mrs. Oakes, don't you know who this gentleman is˙?

MRS. OAKES. No.

DORIS. Come here, and then tell me if you don't recognize him.

(MRS. OAKES *comes from behind the counter and stares at* PETER.)

MRS. OAKES (*at length*). No, I can't say I do.

DORIS. Look again. Look at him sideview. (*To* PETER.) Do you mind turning round ?

PETER (*embarrassed*). I think if you don't mind——

DORIS. There ! You must know that smile. Whom does it remind you of ?

MRS. OAKES (*at length*). Mabel Smart's brother.

PETER. I think I'd better tell you my name straight away, otherwise this might go on all night. I'm Peter Kyle.

MRS. OAKES. Peter Kyle ?

DORIS. The film actor.

MRS. OAKES. An actor ?

DORIS (*frenziedly*). You must have seen him, Mrs. Oakes. He's at The Palace this week in " Light of Love."

MRS. OAKES. I don't go to The Palace. (*To* PETER.) Have you been at the Odeon in Skillingworth ?

PETER. I've really no idea.

DORIS. Of course he has. He's very famous—so please, Mrs. Oakes, do try and fix him up, if you can.

MRS. OAKES (*to* PETER). How long did you want to stay ?

PETER. Just the one night.

MRS. OAKES. Just the one night. (*She crosses behind the counter.*) Well, Countess, seeing that the gentleman is a friend of yours, I'll see what I can do.

PETER. That's terribly kind of you.

MRS. OAKES. Now, let me see. (*She opens the book of rooms.*) I could put up a bed for him in the attic—only I don't like to do that because of fire bombs.

PETER. I don't mind——

MRS. OAKES. No, but I do. I don't want my hotel burnt down.

PETER. But I'm not particularly inflammable.

MRS. OAKES. Possibly not—but the bed is. (*She shuts the book.*) I know. There's Number Twelve. Wing-Commander Taylor. He's Duty Defence Officer, so he'll be sleeping up at the station to-night. You can go in there. (*She opens the register.*) Will you register, please ? And fill in this form.

(PETER *crosses to the desk.* DORIS *comes down* C.)

PETER. I'll fill in the form and give it to you later. (*He fills in the book.*)

MRS. OAKES. I can't send you up at once, because the Wing-Commander might want to use his room before dinner.

PETER. That's quite all right.

MRS. OAKES. You must be careful not to touch any of the Wing-Commander's things. He's most particular. Oh. (*She examines the book.*) I see you're an alien.

(DORIS *sits on the* R. *arm of the sofa.*)

PETER (*nervously*). Er—yes I am——

MRS. OAKES (*coldly*). Dinner is at half-past seven.

(*She goes into her office.*)

PETER (*hangs up his hat and coat*). Evidently she thinks I'm a spy.

DORIS. Oh no, I'm sure she doesn't. It's only that we get so few civilians round here. There's only the aerodrome, you see, and nothing else at all. We're all Air Force here, you know. I suppose you came to see someone up at the station.

PETER. Well—I——

DORIS. I don't want to be inquisitive. I mean, curiosity killed the cat. But I just thought it was such a funny place for a gentleman like you to come to——

PETER (*deliberately, coming down to her,* C.). I was on my way to town. I passed this place and thought it might be fun to stay the night. That's all.

DORIS. Fancy. Well, I'm glad you did, I must say.

PETER (*with automatic gallantry*). So am I.

DORIS (*simpering*). Silly.

Peter (*hastily*). When you say you're Air Force, does that mean you work up at the aerodrome ?

Doris. Oh no. I'm no W.A.A.F. I haven't the figure for it. No—my husband's a pilot.

Peter. Fighter pilot ?

Doris (*shocked*). Oh no. Bombers. Wellingtons. You must have seen them when you passed the aerodrome.

Peter. I'm not very good about aeroplanes——

Doris. Aircraft. Yes, he's captain of a Wellington, is my Johnny. He's done quite a lot of raids. He's only got a few to go before they give him a rest.

Peter. A rest ?

Doris (*crosses to the fireplace for her bag*). Yes. After a fixed number of operational trips they get given a rest, you know— put on to something different—like teaching or groundwork. (*She delves in her bag.*) Will you have a cigarette, Mr. Kyle ?

(*Effects Cue No. 5 : Bombers fade in from a distance.*)

I've got something here called Summer Crop. They're pretty awful, but it's all they've got here. (*She comes back c. and puts her bag on the c. table.*)

Peter. You have one of these. They're Chesterfields.

Doris. Oo, lovely, I will. (*She takes one.*) However did you get them ?

Peter. I smuggled over two thousand in with me from America.

Doris. Naughty ! Do come and sit down and tell me all about Hollywood. Do you know Carmen Miranda or Bing Crosby ?

(*They sit on the sofa.*)

(*Effect Cue No. 6 : Bombers overhead, then fade.*)

(*The aircraft pass overhead. The noise is momentarily very loud.*
Peter *looks up.*)

Peter. What are they ?

Doris (*casually*). Stirlings, I expect. They're four-engine aircraft, anyway. Probably from Shepley. Been a daylight do most likely. The boys'll know. Tell me, did you meet Carmen Miranda or Bing Crosby ?

(*The noise of the bombers fades.*)

Peter. I've never met Carmen Miranda, but I know Bing Crosby fairly well.

Doris. Fancy ! Whatever's he like ?

(*Effects Cue No. 7 : Damaged bomber overhead.*)

(*This time it is* Doris *who looks up.*)

PETER. He's very nice. As a matter of fact our houses are quite near each other and——

DORIS (*sharply*). Sh! (*She jumps up and listens intently.*) There's something wrong with that one.

(*Effects Cue No 8: Damaged bomber landing.*)

(*She runs to the window, opens it and sticks her head out.* PETER *follows her.*)

There she is! See.

PETER (*looking out*). Yes. God, what an enormous thing. It looks all right to me.

DORIS. She's flying on three engines. Been shot up, I expect.

(*The sound passes into the distance.*)

(*Suddenly.*) Oh lor!

PETER. What's the matter?

DORIS. She's landing. Look. They've put the under-carriage down. She's going to land on our aerodrome.

PETER. My God, so it is. It's coming in.

(*Effects Cue No. 9: Engines of bomber off.*)

(PETER *stares intently out of the window. The sound of the aircraft engines fades suddenly as they are throttled back.* DORIS *turns quickly away from the window.*)

DORIS. Is she down?

PETER. Yes. I think so. It's gone out of sight behind those hangars.

(*Effects Cue No. 10: Damaged bomber taxi-ing back.*)

(DORIS *is still listening intently. There comes the sound of the aircraft engines.*)

DORIS. It's all right. She's taxi-ing back.

PETER. It was in trouble all right. It was flying all lopsided.

DORIS. Probably flown by the famous Chinese pilot—Wun Wing Low.

(*Effects Cue No. 11: Taxi-ing back fades.*)

(*She sits on the sofa again. She titters expectantly, but* PETER *does not laugh.*)

Not my joke. Teddy Graham's—he's a flight-loot up at the station. Oo—I've suddenly thought—you must know Mrs. Graham—Teddy Graham's wife—Patricia Warren—the actress, you know. She was in a play of yours in New York. The part was only a—cough and a spit, she says, but you might remember her. She's staying here.

PETER (*sitting by her*). Really?

Doris. Do you remember her ?

Peter. Yes, I do.

Doris. She's ever so nice, I think. Don't you ?

Peter. Yes. Charming.

Doris. She won't half be surprised when she sees you. She went up for a nap. Shall I call her down ?

Peter. No, please don't. I'll see her later, anyway.

Doris. She's only been here since yesterday morning. It's the first chance she's had of coming to see her hubby as the play she was acting in in London only came off last week. He's just been made captain of a Wellington—she's as proud as proud of him. It's a treat to see them together—it is really.

Peter (*abruptly*). I feel it's time for a drink. Can I get you one ?

Doris. Thank you, Mr. Kyle. I'll have a gin-and-lime. There's the bell by the door.

(Peter *presses a bell. A man in the uniform of a Sergeant Air Gunner comes in from the road. He is about thirty-five, small, dark and insignificant. His name is* David Miller *and he is known, naturally, as* Dusty.)

Dusty. 'Evening, Countess.

Doris. Hullo, Dusty.

Dusty. Spotted my wife anywhere ?

Doris. I don't think she's come yet, Dusty. She was coming by 'bus, wasn't she ?

Dusty. Four-twenty-five from Lincoln—so she should 'ave been 'ere twenty minutes ago. She's a proper mucker-upper, though—she'll go and catch the wrong 'bus, you see—end up in Grimsby and then blame me. (*While he is speaking he is taking off his overcoat. He now turns and sees* Peter.) Oh, excuse me—— (*Down* R.C.)

Peter (*crossing to* Dusty). We were just going to have a drink. Will you join us ?

Dusty. Thank you, sir. I don't mind.

Peter. I've rung the bell, but nothing seems to happen. (*To* Dusty.) What does A.G. stand for ?

Dusty⎱ (*together*). Air gunner.
Doris⎰

Doris. Didn't you know that ? You are ignorant.

Peter. Yes, I am, I'm afraid. So you're the man who sits in the rear turret ?

Dusty. That's right. Tail-end stooge—that's me.

Peter. What's it like being a tail-end stooge ?

Dusty. Oh, not so bad. Gets a bit cold sometimes.

Peter. A bit cold is an understatement, isn't it ?

Dusty. Don't know. Depends, really. Some nights it's all

right. Other nights you come down and you got to get a bloke with a 'ammer and chisel to get you off of the seat.

(*A boy of about fifteen* (PERCY), *wearing an apron, comes through the door marked Lounge.*)

PERCY. Anybody ring ?

PETER (*going down to him*). Yes, I rang. I want a gin-and-lime—— (*To* DUSTY.) What's yours ?

DUSTY. Beer please, sir.

PETER. A beer and a whisky-and-soda.

PERCY (*with a broad smile*). There's no whisky.

PETER. Then I'll have a gin and tonic.

PERCY (*with a broader smile*). There's no tonic.

PETER. Then bring me a pink gin.

PERCY (*disappointed*). Yes, you can have that. (*To* DUSTY.) Was that a Stirling come down 'bout ten minutes ago, Sergeant?

DUSTY. That's none of your business what it was, nosey.

PERCY. Garn, I knows a Stirling when I seen one. Anyone hurt inside ?

DUSTY (*with dignity*). I've no idea, I'm sure.

PERCY (*with relish*). Bet there was. I saw an ambulance driving out.

(*He recognizes* PETER. *He goes out shouting,* " Fred, do you know who's here ? ")

DORIS. Was anyone hurt ?

(DUSTY *crosses to her and nods.*)

Bad ?

DUSTY. Two bumped off—tail gunner and wireless op. Cannon shells. Other gunner caught it—not bad though.

DORIS. Been a daylight do, has there ?

DUSTY. Big one. (*With a glance at* PETER.) Talk about careless talk !

DORIS. Oh, don't mind him. You don't know who he is, do you ?

DUSTY. No. Can't say I do.

DORIS. It's Peter Kyle.

DUSTY (*after a pause*). Cor ! (*He gazes awestruck at* PETER.)

PETER (*going up to him*). What's *your* name, Sergeant ?

DUSTY. Miller, sir.

PETER. I'm glad to meet you. (*He shakes hands.*)

DUSTY. Peter Kyle. Well, I'm a—— Do you know Dorothy Lamour ?

PETER. No. I can't say I do.

DUSTY (*plainly disappointed*). Oh.

(PERCY *comes in with the drinks on a tray.*)

PERCY (*crossing to* DORIS, *hands her a drink*).   It *was* a Stirling come down.   Fred in the bar seen 'er too.   (*He turns to* DUSTY.)

DUSTY (*takes drink and crosses behind the sofa*).   Fred in the bar can be wrong, sometimes, I presume, or is he omnificent ?

PERCY (*hands the tray to* PETER).   I don't know what he is, but 'e knows it was a Stirling.   Shot up something terrible it was 'e says.

(PETER *pays him.*)

PETER.   Keep the change.

PERCY (*surprised*).   Thank you, sir.   Thank you.   (*He crosses* PETER *to the door.*)   Where's it to-night, Sergeant, Berlin ?

DUSTY.   It'll be a clip on the ear'ole for you, my lad, if I 'ave any more of your lip.   Beat it !

(PERCY *goes.   His voice can be heard in the lounge before the door closes behind him.*)

PERCY (*off*).   Sergeant says it's Berlin to-night.

DORIS (*to* DUSTY, *in a low voice*).   Nothing on to-night, is there, dear ?

DUSTY (*down* L. *of the sofa*).   Not as far as I know.

DORIS (*cheerfully*).   Tinkerty tonk, Mr. Kyle !

PETER (*leaning against the counter*).   Good health.

(*They drink.   A Flying Officer* (COUNT SKRICZEVINSKY) *comes in. He wears the Polish air force eagle over the left breast, and the word " Poland " on his shoulders.   He is over forty, tall and thin, with a permanent and slightly bewildered smile.   He hangs up his hat and gasmask.*)

DORIS (*rising, goes up to him at the door*).   Hullo, Johnny ducks, you're early.   (*She kisses him lightly on the cheek, and brings him down to* PETER.)   Is Teddy with you ?

COUNT.   'E—poots—car—garage.   (*He speaks English with the greatest difficulty, always retaining his bewildered expression.*)

DUSTY.   'Evening, sir.

COUNT.   Good—evening.

DORIS.   Johnny, I want you to meet a very famous man.

COUNT.   Pardon ?

DORIS (*pointing at* PETER).   Very—famous—man.   Film star. Understand ?   Peter Kyle.

COUNT (*not having understood*).   Oh yes—please.

PETER.   How do you do ?

(*He shakes hands.   The* COUNT *clicks his heels slightly.*)

DORIS.   Isn't he sweet when he does that ?   First time I met him, he kissed my hand.   Of course, I had to fall for him after that, didn't I, Johnny ducks ?

(*The* COUNT *smiles at her vaguely and she squeezes his hand.*)

You must excuse his English, Mr. Kyle. It's not up to much but it's getting better. He's having English lessons up at the station—aren't you, Johnny ducks ?

Count. Please ?

Dusty. English—lessons, sir. Your wife says you are having English lessons.

Count (*with a sudden burst of loquacity*). Oh yes. English lessons. I learn much. 'Ow are you to-day, Mrs. Brown, please ? Se Eiffel Tower is se towellest beelding in se vurruld.

Doris. World, Johnny, world. Not vurruld.

Count. World. World.

(Mrs. Oakes *appears at the office door. She puts a telegram in the letter rack.* Doris *crosses to the sofa and sits on the* l. *arm.*)

Mrs. Oakes. Good evening, Count.

Count. Good evening, Missus.

Mrs. Oakes. You'll be in to dinner, I presume ?

Count. Oh yes, sank you, please.

Mrs. Oakes. And you'll be staying the night ? No early breakfasts or late suppers ? (*She winks heavily.*)

Count. No, please. To-night I stye wiss my vife.

(Mrs. Oakes *picks up her room-book and starts to go.*)

Doris (*to the* Count). Not stye. Stay. To-night I stay with my wife.

Dusty (*calling*). Oh, Mrs. Oakes !

(Mrs. Oakes *turns.*)

Mrs. Oakes. Yes ?

Dusty. It's all right about that double room for to-night, isn't it ?

Mrs. Oakes. Yes. You've got Number Two. Do you want to go up now ?

Dusty. No, thanks. The wife's not come yet. Should 've been 'ere near an hour ago. (*Gloomily.*) Just like her, I will say. (*He crosses to the fire.*)

Mrs. Oakes. She'll turn up—you'll find.

(*She disappears as* Teddy Graham *comes in through the front door. He is a Flight-Lieutenant and wears the D.F.C. His age is 24.*)

Teddy (*coming down to* Doris). Hullo, Doris, my beautiful. How's every little thing ?

Doris. Mustn't grumble.

Teddy. 'Evening, Sergeant. Where's the wife ?

Dusty (*crosses* c. *slightly*). Don't know, sir. Gone off course a bit—looks like.

(TEDDY *takes off his hat and coat and goes up to hang them up.*)

TEDDY.   You told me her navigation was pretty ropey.

DUSTY.   It's lousy.   If she don't come soon I'd post her as missing—believed got in the wrong 'bus.   (*He goes back to the fire.*)

TEDDY.   I should.   Johnny, you clot!   What about that beer you were going to get me ?

COUNT.   I not forget.

(*He rings the bell.*   TEDDY *suddenly sees* PETER *and approaches him cautiously.*)

TEDDY.   Good God!   It's—not—Peter Kyle—is it ?

DORIS (*rises and goes up to* TEDDY).   Yes, it is, Teddy.   It really is.   Isn't it wonderful ?

TEDDY.   Pukka gen ?

DORIS.   Pukka gen.   (*She goes down to the* R. *end of the sofa.*)

TEDDY.   Good Lord!   I say—I mean—Good Lord!   I say, I'm most awfully glad to meet you, sir, and all that.

PETER.   Must you call me sir ?

TEDDY.   No, I suppose not—I mean—Peter Kyle!   Well, well, well!   (*He shakes* PETER'S *hand energetically.*)   This calls for a party, don't you think, boys and girls ?   (*Calling.*)   Percy !

COUNT (*going up to* TEDDY).   Please—I wish——

TEDDY.   All right, Johnny—these are mine.   (*He pushes him over to* DORIS.   *Pointing at* PETER.)   Very famous bloke here, Johnny.

COUNT.   Oh yes, sank you.

(PERCY *appears promptly, his manner, when he speaks to* TEDDY, *surprisingly deferential.*)

PERCY.   Yes, Flight-Lieutenant Graham, sir ?

TEDDY.   Where have *you* been ?   We've been ringing for half an hour.

PERCY.   Sorry, sir.   Didn't know it was you, Flight-Lieutenant Graham, sir.

TEDDY.   Another round for these people whatever they're having, Percy, and pints for the Count and me.

PERCY.   Yes, sir.   Berlin to-night, Flight-Lieutenant Graham, sir ?

TEDDY.   What ?   No, Percy.   Home Sweet Home, to-night.

(PERCY'S *face falls.   He goes out, down* R.)

I say, this has rather shaken me—you know—I mean your being here, in the old Falcon—just like—I mean—a commercial traveller or something.   No offence, or anything——

PETER.   That's all right.

TEDDY. Good Lord, you must know Pat. (*He crosses to the foot of the stairs above the sofa.*) That's my wife. Patricia Warren she was—still is—I mean she still uses the name and all that. (*Calling.*) Pat! Pat! Are you upstairs?

(PETER *comes down* R.)

PATRICIA (*her voice coming from upstairs*). Hullo, Teddy. I heard you come in.

TEDDY. Come on down. There's something down here that's going to shake you considerably.

PATRICIA. Oh? Just coming.

TEDDY (*crossing below the sofa to* PETER R.). I say, I suppose you do know her. I mean, she was in a play of yours, you know—tiny part, but she shoots a line about your having been very kind to her and all that——

PETER. Does she? Yes, I remember her well.

TEDDY. Look—you go there (*he pushes him to up* L. *directly beneath the stairs*)—so she won't see you as she comes down——

PETER (*protestingly*). No, I think——

DORIS (*pushing him also*). Go on, silly! Look out!

(TEDDY *goes behind the sofa.* DORIS *leans on the left banister.* PATRICIA GRAHAM *comes down the stairs. She is about* TEDDY'S *age, perhaps a year or two older.*)

PATRICIA. What's all this about my being shaken?

TEDDY. Nothing, darling. Just to get you to come down.

PATRICIA. Hullo, Johnny. Good evening, Doris.

TEDDY (*coming down level with* DUSTY). This is Sergeant Miller—my tail gunner. A very bad type——

PATRICIA (*comes down to him at the fire and shakes hands*). He doesn't look it. How do you do? (*Brightly, turning to* TEDDY.) It's funny the loose way you Air Force people use your slang. For instance, to shake someone or to be shaken seems to cover anything from crashing in flames to seeing a caterpillar or, something——

(DORIS *pushes* PETER *down to the* L. *of* PATRICIA. PATRICIA *turns. She stands quite still.* PETER *smiles, but she does not smile in return. She turns her head quickly to look at* TEDDY, *who is gazing at her, smiling expectantly. Then she looks back at* PETER.)

PETER. Hullo.

PATRICIA. Hullo.

(*They shake hands.*)

TEDDY. Well, darling, are you shaken or are you shaken? Now be honest.

PATRICIA. I'll be honest. I'm shaken.

(PERCY *comes in, staggering under the weight of a loaded tray. He puts it on a table down* R. PATRICIA *crosses to the table* R.)

Which of these is for me ?

TEDDY (*following her*). Well—as a matter of fact——

PATRICIA. Teddy—you don't mean to tell me you've left me out. I'll have a pink gin.

TEDDY. Another pink gin, Percy.

PERCY. Yes, sir.

TEDDY. Come on, everybody. (*He takes three beers. He gives one to the* COUNT *behind the sofa and then to* DUSTY *at the fire.*)

(PERCY *goes out.* PETER *crosses to the table.* JOHNNY *comes down slightly.* PETER *takes up the drinks for* DORIS *and himself.*)

PATRICIA. When did you arrive ?

DORIS (*crossing to* PETER). Only a few minutes ago. Just fancy Peter Kyle blowing into the old Falcon just like that. Happened to be passing and thought it would be fine to stay the night. You should have seen my face. (*She takes her drink from* PETER.)

PATRICIA (*brightly*). Yes. (*Crossing* L. *to* TEDDY.) What's the news from the aerodrome, Teddy ?

TEDDY. Nothing much. (*Raising his glass.*) Cheers, everybody !

(DORIS *goes up to* JOHNNY.)

PATRICIA. There must be some news or are you going all careless talk on me ?

TEDDY. First time I've ever known you take an interest in what's going on at the aerodrome. As a matter of fact it's been a quiet day, hasn't it, Sarge ?

DUSTY. Pretty quiet, sir.

TEDDY. A Stirling force-landed a few minutes ago. You probably saw it.

PETER. The Countess and I saw it.

(PATRICIA *sits on the* L. *arm of the sofa.*)

DORIS. Don't call me Countess, please, Mr. Kyle. Or if you do, give me my full name, which is Countess Skriczevinsky.

(*She screws her face up in a mock effort to pronounce the name.*)

COUNT (*correcting her gently*). Please Countess Skriczevinsky.

DORIS. Get Johnny correcting me for a change !

(*There is a general laugh. The* COUNT *looks slightly more bewildered.*)

B

(*Correctly.*) Sorry, ducks, I can say it, Johnny. I was only fooling, Countess Skriczevinsky.

(*The* Count *smiles.*)

Patricia. What was the matter with the Stirling that force-landed ?

Teddy. Been shot up in a raid. Big raid too, I believe. I can't tell you where, of course.

(Percy *comes in with* Patricia's *pink gin and puts it on the* c. *table.*)

Percy. 'Ell of a do on Kiel this afternoon.

Teddy (*startled*). Come here, Percy. (*Regarding* Percy *sternly, as he crosses.*) Who told you that ?

Percy. Just come through on the six o'clock. (*He crosses to the door.*)

Teddy. Oh, the laugh's on me.

Percy. 'Ell of a do it must 'ave been. Blenheims, Wimpeys, 'Alifaxes and Stirlings. We lost seventeen. Shot down twenty-two of theirs, though.

(*He goes out.* Doris *sits on the* c. *table and hands* Patricia *her drink.*)

Teddy. Seventeen ? Not too good. (*He meets* Dusty's *eye.*) I reckon the squadron's done pretty well up to now to keep out of these daylight do's, don't you ?

Dusty (*fervently*). You're telling me.

Count (*suddenly*). I—have—wish to go on sese daylight do's.

Teddy. You mean, you don't have wish.

Count. No, no. I *do* have wish. I have wish to see my bombs to fall——

(*There is a slight pause.*)

Teddy. I see what you mean, Johnny old boy.

(Doris *takes his hand.* Patricia *drains her glass.*)

Patricia. I want another drink.

Teddy. Good Lord ! You haven't finished that one already ?

Patricia. Yes, I have.

Peter (*calling at the door*). Percy !

(Percy *appears at the door.*)

(*Politely.*) What were you drinking, Mrs. Graham ?

Patricia. Thank you, Mr. Kyle. It was a pink gin.

Peter. A pink gin for Mrs. Graham—and the same again for the others. (*He is behind the table* r.)

(Percy *goes out.*)

DORIS. My Johnny'll be getting tinky-boo. He can't stand more than a couple, can you, ducks ?

COUNT. Yes, please.

DORIS. He means, no thank you.

COUNT. No, sank you.

DORIS. Thank you, Johnny. Thank. Th-ank.

COUNT. Sank you. Sank you.

TEDDY. Good old Johnny. Keep cracking—it'll come.

(PERCY *comes in with new short drinks.* *He puts them on the table*
R. *and exits.*)

PERCY (*off*). Hurry up with those pints, Fred.

TEDDY. Just as well we've got to-night at home, eh, Dusty ?

(PETER *hands* DORIS *her gin and lime, then crosses behind the sofa
and gives* PATRICIA *the pink gin.*)

DUSTY (*gloomily*). I wouldn't put it past 'em to send us out now. They done it before.

TEDDY (*sits on the arm of the chair above the fire*). Dusty's the world's prize moaner. He even moaned to me over the inter-comm. because he'd shot down a Messerschmitt. Tell them about it, Dusty.

DUSTY (*alarmed*). No, Mr. Graham, sir, please. Not now.

PATRICIA (*politely*). Do tell us, Sergeant.

(PETER *puts the tray on the window seat and stands behind the
sofa.*)

DUSTY. It's nothing, Mum, really. Mr. Graham's told you it's only I shot down a Messerschmitt, I think.

TEDDY. What do you mean, you think ? It was at night, Patricia. Nothing else in the sky for miles around except us and this one-one-o, and he still thinks someone else might have shot it down. Tell 'em, Dusty.

DUSTY. They'll think it's a line, sir.

PATRICIA. Why don't *you* tell the story, Teddy ?

TEDDY. I didn't see it. We were stooge-ing along over the Dutch coast somewhere, and suddenly I hear Dusty's voice over the intercomm., saying : (*imitating* DUSTY's *gloomy voice*) " 'Ullo, skipper. Tail calling. M.E. one-one-o's just been at us. Sod's gone into the drink on fire. Over."

(*There is a general laugh.* DUSTY *looks acutely uncomfortable.*)

" Gone " is the operative word.

(PERCY *comes in with the beers and stands by* JOHNNY, *listening.*)

PATRICIA (*to* DUSTY). You did shoot at it, though, didn't you ?

DUSTY. Oh yes, Mum. I shot at it all right. Bright moon there was. Saw it as clear as I'm seeing you. He opens up 'bout five 'undred yards with 'is cannons, and I've got 'im in my sights, and 'e's getting bigger all the time, and I press the triggers and there's a ruddy great glow all of a sudden and down 'e goes into the drink turning and twisting. I thought——

(*There is a pause. Everyone, including the* COUNT, *is listening intently.*)

Crikey !

PATRICIA. That's not what I'd have thought.

(*The* COUNT *takes a drink from* PERCY. *Enter* MAUDIE *up* R., *at the front door. She is a small woman, much muffled up, and carries a small case, umbrella, and gas-mask. She comes down* R.)

DUSTY. First time I'd ever seen a Messerschmitt, and down he goes—just like that. (*He clicks his teeth unbelievingly.*)

TEDDY. Good show, Dusty. (*He takes a beer for himself and* DUSTY.) You get another beer for that. (*He sees* MAUDIE.) Oh, Dusty——

(DUSTY *puts down his beer and crosses to her.*)

DUSTY. 'Ullo, Maudie.

MAUDIE. Hullo, Dave.

(*They do not kiss.* PETER, DORIS *and* JOHNNY *have gone up to the window, and have politely turned their backs.*)

DUSTY. Got on the wrong 'bus, did you, Maudie ?

(TEDDY *and* PATRICIA *talk together.* PATRICIA *sits on the sofa.*)

MAUDIE (*accusingly*). You said the Skillingworth 'bus, Dave.

DUSTY. Yes, that's right. Four-twenty-five from Lincoln.

MAUDIE. Well, I went to Skillingworth and you weren't there.

DUSTY. Lor, Maudie, I didn't tell you to go to Skillingworth. You should 'ave got off at Milchester.

MAUDIE (*still accusingly*). You said the Skillingworth 'bus, Dave.

DUSTY. Yes, but the Skillingworth 'bus goes through Milchester : you should 'ave got off at Milchester.

MAUDIE. You never said nothing about Milchester. You don't look very well, Dave. Have you been getting those backaches ?

(DUSTY *looks round hurriedly at the others. Only* TEDDY *is looking at him.*)

DUSTY (*hastily*). Here, Maudie ! You sign your name here.

MAUDIE (*Putting down her case. Not to be put off*). Because if you have, I've brought that medicine you left behind last leave—the one your doctor gave you——

DUSTY. All right, Maudie. Here's where you sign. Here. (*He pushes her over to the counter where she signs her name.*)

TEDDY (*crossing to* DUSTY). So she got in to base at last, Dusty.

DUSTY. Yes, sir, I brought her in on the beam.

TEDDY. How do you do, Mrs. Miller ?

(*They shake hands.*)

DUSTY. This is Flight-Lieutenant Graham, Maudie—you know—the one I was telling you about. He's my skipper.

MAUDIE. Pleased to meet you.

TEDDY. How do you think he's looking ?

MAUDIE. A bit peaky, I told him : I think he must have been getting those backaches of his——

DUSTY (*hastily, picking up her case*). If you'll excuse us, sir, we'll be nipping upstairs——

TEDDY. See you both later.

(DUSTY *shepherds* MAUDIE *across the room to the stairs.*)

MAUDIE (*as they go*). The man at Skillingworth said I should have caught the four-forty-five from Lincoln.

DUSTY (*heatedly*). He doesn't know what he's talking about. Four-twenty-five's all right, if you done what I told you——

MAUDIE. He said the four-forty-five doesn't go through Skillingworth at all, and all I had to do was to change into a Milchester 'bus at Windowbrook—you did say the Skillingworth 'bus, Dave.

(*They pass out of sight.*)

PETER. The henpecked hero.

(DORIS *moves down* R.C.)

DORIS (*picking up her bag off the* C. *table*).‧ Dusty's not henpecked, believe me. I bet he gives as good as he gets. Shall *we* go upstairs, Johnny ducks.

(JOHNNY *comes down to her* L. *of the sofa.*)

I must tidy up a bit and dinner's quite soon and you'll want a shave.

COUNT. Please ?

DORIS. Shave, dear. (*She strokes his chin, as they cross to the stairs.*)

COUNT. Oh yes. Not—shave—sis—morning. Very—pricky.

DORIS. Prickly, duckie.

TEDDY. Perhaps he meant pretty. (*Leaning against the counter.*)

DORIS. He meant prickly—and he's right. I don't like my beautiful going about looking like an old porcupine. Come on, Johnny.

COUNT (*with a great effort*). Yes. Excuse, please. I must go up to my room where I will shave.

TEDDY. Terrific, Johnny! Well done!

COUNT (*delighted*). That was good how I am saying him?

DORIS. Yes, my precious, but that wasn't. That was ruddy awful how you were saying him.

(*They pass out of sight.*)

TEDDY. Talk about henpecking—Doris rules her old Count with a rod of iron.

(*There is a pause. Neither PATRICIA nor PETER answer him. PATRICIA rises and crosses to the fire.*)

PETER (*coming down behind the sofa*). What's that? I'm sorry.

TEDDY (*crosses to him slightly*). I said Doris rules her old Count with a rod of iron.

(*PATRICIA finishes her drink and sits on the fender.*)

PETER. Yes. I feel awfully sorry for him.

TEDDY. Why? Doris is all right.

PETER. Yes. She seems charming. Only—well, of course, it may just be that he doesn't speak any English.

TEDDY. Even if he didn't speak a word of English I don't think he'd run any risk of mistaking Doris for the Duchess of Dillwater.

PETER. No, I suppose not. How long have they been married?

TEDDY. I don't know. He was married to her when they formed the Polish Squadron on the station. He's good value, old Johnny. (*He finishes his beer and puts his glass on the c. table.*) I'm going to have a bath before dinner. (*He strolls to the stairs.*) I'm sure you two are longing to get down to a nice theatrical gossip match.

PETER. We'll have quite a lot to talk about, I expect.

TEDDY (*on the stairs*). I bet you will. All about Angel Fanny and Sweetie-pie Cyril. Darling, can I borrow your eau-de-Cologne?

PATRICIA. Yes, but don't take too much—it's absolutely priceless.

TEDDY. I'm going to pour it on with a bucket. If I can't look like the screen's great lover, I can at least smell like a glamour boy. So long.

(*He goes out of sight, whistling.   There is a pause.*)

PETER (*moving down* R.C.).   He's nice, but what a baby.

(PATRICIA *rises, looking angrily at him.*)

Darling, don't be angry, please.

PATRICIA.   Angry ?

PETER (*crossing to her,* C.).   I don't see that I've done anything so wrong in coming down to face the music.

PATRICIA (L.C.).   Face the music ?   How beautifully Hollywood !   What was your idea ?   To get Teddy alone and say " I love your wife " ?

PETER.   If you must know, yes.

PATRICIA (*bitterly*).   How did you visualize the scene after that ?   (*Crossing him to the table* R.).   Was it like your last film when you let Spencer Tracy knock you down, and saved each other's lives just before the fade out ?   (*She turns to him.*)   And you call Teddy a baby !

PETER (*stubbornly, following her*).   I'm sorry but I've never been able to see why you should have to do the telling alone.

PATRICIA.   Because this isn't a film, and there's no need for you to worry about whether you're playing a sympathetic part.

PETER.   You're being rather brutal.

PATRICIA (*near tears*).   I'm trying to be.

PETER.   Pat, darling.

(PATRICIA *turns quickly away to face* R., PETER *staring at her bewildered.*)

This hasn't made any difference, has it ?

PATRICIA (*turning back to face* L.).   Of course it hasn't made any difference.

PETER (*after a pause*).   I'll go away to-night.   (*He crosses below the sofa to the armchair* L.C.)

PATRICIA.   What's the use ?   He's seen you and spoken to you.   He's heard us calling each other Mr. Kyle and Mrs. Graham.   You've quite quietly reduced the whole thing to the level of a rather nasty little intrigue.

PETER (*obstinately*).   You'd much better let me tell him.   I can explain——

PATRICIA (*violently, crossing to* C.).   I'm the one to tell him—the only one, Pete.

(PETER *looks at her in silence, then shrugs his shoulders and turns away.   There is a pause.   Then* PATRICIA *crosses to him and puts her hand on his arm.*)

(*a change of tone*).   I'm sorry, darling.   I am hating all this, you see.

PETER.   I know.   Are you sure I can't help ?

PATRICIA. I'm afraid you can't. Nobody can.

PETER. What are you going to tell him ?

PATRICIA. Everything.

PETER. Starting way back ?

PATRICIA. Way back. (*She crosses to the fire.*) It *is* way back, I suppose ?

PETER. April the twenty-seventh, nineteen-thirty-eight.

PATRICIA. You always did have a date complex.

PETER. So did you. What about our celebrations on the twenty-seventh of every month ? You can't have forgotten them ? (*He moves to her.*)

PATRICIA (*nodding*). Fifteen altogether.

PETER. I wish you'd told him that part of it when you married him. Then this wouldn't be so difficult now.

PATRICIA. In films the wife always tells her husband about her past affairs—doesn't she ?

PETER. Shut up about films, darling.

(*They look upstairs.* PATRICIA *crosses to the sofa and sits.*)

Why didn't you tell him ? Funk ? (*He leans over the* L. *end of the sofa.*)

PATRICIA. No, I didn't see why I should.

PETER. Yes, but I still think it would have been better——

PATRICIA. If I'd told him anything about you at all, I'd have had to admit that I was still in love with you when I married him—and that was something I didn't want to admit even to myself.

(*A pause.*)

PETER. You *were* a fool to run out on me, weren't you ?

PATRICIA. You *were* a fool to let me go.

PETER. Well, I couldn't very well have stopped you, could I ?

PATRICIA (*takes his hand*). You could have come over here a bit sooner than you did. I couldn't go to you after the war had started—or a letter would have been rather nice.

PETER. I was making a big experiment, darling, you know that—trying to live without you. It wasn't a success.

PATRICIA. Nor was mine.

(*A pause.* PETER *looks at her for a moment, withdraws his hand, and then turns away.*)

PETER (*in a deliberately casual voice*). When you married Teddy, how much did you feel for him ?

PATRICIA. I don't know, he didn't give me much chance. He was on a week's leave, and we were married before he went back to his squadron. What the papers would call a whirlwind wartime romance.

PETER (*moves back to her*). But now you do know, don't you ?
PATRICIA. Yes, I know now.
PETER. Tell me, then, how much do you feel for him now ?
(PATRICIA *smiles*.) I'm horribly jealous of him. You know that.
PATRICIA. I'd be angry if you weren't. You can't know anyone as well as I know Teddy without feeling something for them, and something rather strong.
PETER. Is there much to know ?
PATRICIA. Not much—but what there is, is—well—just terribly nice. (*After a slight pause*.) But in the sense which you mean, I don't feel anything for him at all.
PETER. That's true, isn't it, Pat ?
PATRICIA. Yes, it's true. I'd have given quite a lot to have said to you the other day, go back to America, Mr. Kyle, I'm married and in love, and I don't want you. It's a pity I couldn't, isn't it ?
PETER. I suppose you might say it's a pity for both of us, but somehow I don't think that's true.

(*They look at each other.   Then* PETER *walks away towards the fire*.)

You won't run out on me again, will you ?
PATRICIA. You know why I did, don't you ?
PETER. Because of the row——
PATRICIA. Not because of the row. If it hadn't been over that, it would have been over something else. I ran out purely and simply because I couldn't bear not being married to you.
PETER (*laughing*). Considering we'd been living—as you might say—in sin—for well over a year——
PATRICIA. I know. But you see, even after we'd been living together for months and months, people still behaved to me as the latest Peter Kyle girl friend. I hated Rita for not giving you a divorce. In the end it made me so frightened of losing you that I ran away from you. D'you understand that ?
PETER. No.
PATRICIA (*smiling*). Of course you don't. It's mad, isn't it ?
PETER (*crossing back to her*). Absolutely batty—anyway, now that Rita has given in——
PATRICIA. Don't worry, darling. All the Ritas in the world wouldn't get me to make the same mistake again—or any mistake again. (*After a pause*.) I'll tell Teddy to-night. Ring the bell, I want another drink.

(PETER *does so and comes* R.C.)

(*Lighting Cue No. 1 : Light starts to fade*.)

PETER. Why didn't you tell him last night ?
PATRICIA. There was a party. They were all very sweet, and they all had gallons of beer, and they all sang songs, very bawdy

most of them—and finally two or three of them passed out like
logs.

PETER. What about Teddy ? Did he pass out too ?

PATRICIA. Yes. I had to put him to bed, poor lamb.

PETER. Charming for you.

PATRICIA. No, it wasn't—yes, it was, rather.

PETER. It couldn't have been.

PATRICIA. I don't know. I quite enjoyed it. I was so
relieved that I hadn't got to tell him.

(*Enter* PERCY.)

PERCY. You rang ?

PETER. Yes, Percy. I want a pink gin for Mrs. Graham.

PERCY. Coo ! That's the third, isn't it ?

PETER. Yes, Percy. That's the third.

PERCY. Coo ! (*He turns to go.*)

(TEDDY *appears on the landing, smoking a cigarette.*)

TEDDY. Hey ! Percy ! (*To the others.*) You've ordered,
haven't you ?

PETER. Yes, we have.

TEDDY. Get me a beer. (*He comes down to the fire and looks
in the mirror.*)

PERCY. O.K., Flight-Lieutenant Graham, sir.

(*He goes out.*)

PATRICIA. You've been very quick.

TEDDY. As far as a bath went, I've had it.

PETER (*crossing behind the sofa to* TEDDY). You had a
bath ?

TEDDY. No. The water was cold.

PETER. But you said you had it.

TEDDY. I had it—meaning I didn't have it.

PETER. How can you have had it when you didn't have it ?
I don't understand.

PATRICIA. You're being very dense. It's Air Force slang.

PETER. Oh, I see. So you're still unbathed ?

TEDDY. Yes, but I smell gorgeous. (*He goes up to* PETER.)
Smell.

PETER. Gorgeous.

TEDDY (*crossing to* PATRICIA *and sitting on the back of the sofa*).
Smell.

PATRICIA. Gorgeous, Teddy.

PETER (*crossing to the counter*). How long have we got before
dinner ? (*He picks up his suitcase.*)

TEDDY. About half an hour, if it's not out on its E.T.A.

PETER. E.T.A. ?

TEDDY. Estimated time of arrival.

PETER. Oh, I see. Well, I think *I'll* go up now. I haven't even seen my room yet. (*He walks up the stairs.*)

TEDDY. Did you have a nice bee, you two ?

PETER (*on the stairs*). Yes, thank you, Teddy. (*He leans over the banisters.*) Do you mind me calling you Teddy ?

TEDDY (*rising, goes up to the banister*). Good Lord, no. It's an honour.

PETER. An honour ? Thank you, Teddy.

(*He goes out.*)

TEDDY (*behind the sofa*). Nice bloke, considering.

PATRICIA. Considering what ?

TEDDY. He's an actor.

PATRICIA (*crossing to the fire*). Thank you for the comment on my profession.

TEDDY (*sits on the back of the sofa*). Darling, don't be a clot.

(PERCY *enters carrying a tray with beer and pink gin. He crosses to the* O. *table, puts down the drinks and starts clearing the empties on to the tray.*)

I didn't mean you. You're the old exception that proves the old rule, if you see what I mean.

PATRICIA. What old rule is that ?

TEDDY. Well, actors are funny blokes. They never seem to be themselves. They only worry about what sort of effect they're having on other people.

PATRICIA. They act—in other words ?

TEDDY. Yes, I suppose that's it. They never seem to do or say anything naturally. They're always thinking of an invisible audience. I bet they even act in the bathroom.

(PERCY, *who has now finished the clearing, goes out giggling.*)

PERCY (*off, in the lounge*). Do you know what Flight-Lieutenant Graham just said ? He said——

(*The door closes.*)

TEDDY. Percy'll get me a bad reputation. Don't you agree, though, darling ?

PATRICIA (*lightly*). Not altogether. I think they feel things like other people—although, I admit, they're inclined to act what they feel rather than just—feel.

(TEDDY *rises, picks up his own and* PATRICIA'S *drink and gives it to her.*)

TEDDY. Oh, well. Perhaps you're right. Don't let's argue anyway. We never have and we never will. (*He raises his glass.*) Cheers, darling.

PATRICIA. Cheers. (*She gulps her drink, makes a wry face and goes up to the banister.*)

TEDDY (*taking her glass*). I say. (*He puts it back on the* C. *table.*) That went down the old hatch pretty quick, didn't it ?

PATRICIA. Teddy——

TEDDY (*crosses* R., *then turns to her*). Darling, I've just thought. Talking about actors acting and all that. We all act, in a way. At least, I know I do.

PATRICIA (*smiling*). Do you, Teddy ?

TEDDY (*seriously*). Yes, I do. I don't mean with you, so much. Up in the mess, with the blokes. They call me P/O Prune—he's a character in " The Training Manual "—sort of crazy, good-tempered, halfwitted sort of bloke—you know the type—and I—well, I kind of act P/O Prune for them. (*He sits on the table* C.) Yesterday for instance, I was up on an air test, and I saw the C.O.'s car pulling out of the gate, so I put the old Wimpey into a dive and beat him up—you know, pulled out only a few feet above his head and stooged round him. I didn't particularly like doing it, and I had the hell of a strip torn off about it afterwards—but—well—I was being P/O Prune, you see, and the blokes had a good laugh.

(PATRICIA *is staring at him from the foot of the stairs. When he finishes she turns her head away quickly.* TEDDY *notices the movement.*)

Sorry. I'm being a bore.

PATRICIA (*uncertainly*). No, you're not. Go on.

TEDDY (*rises*). I say, Pat, is anything the matter ?

PATRICIA (*wipes her eyes quickly and goes up to the window*). Nothing. I'm being an actress, that's all.

TEDDY (*puzzled*). Did I say anything ?

PATRICIA. No. I'm a bit tight, I think. When I'm tight I get weepy. I'm all right, now.

TEDDY. Lesson to me not to talk about myself. I'm ashamed of you, Graham, making a woman cry.

(*There is an awkward pause.*)

Oh, by the way. (*He goes up to her at the window.*) Have you any plans for to-morrow evening ?

PATRICIA (*uncertainly*). No—I—that's to say, I don't think so.

TEDDY. Let's go over to Lincoln and beat up The Saracen's Head a trifle, shall we ?

PATRICIA. If you like.

TEDDY. We might take old Johnny and Doris along with us, too. I've got an idea this hole is getting you down a bit. We'll make a night of it, to-morrow.

PATRICIA (*impulsively*). Teddy——

TEDDY. Yes ?

PATRICIA. I've got something I must tell you.

TEDDY. All right. Don't look so serious about it. What is it ?

PATRICIA. Not here. Shall we go upstairs ? (*She passes him to the foot of the stairs.*)

TEDDY (*following her*). This sounds awful. You look like our C.O. at his worst. Are you going to tear me off a strip ?

(PATRICIA *is already walking up the stairs.*)

PATRICIA. Don't talk, Teddy, please.

TEDDY. I know. You want me to pay a dress bill.

PATRICIA (*violently*). Don't talk !

(*An Air Force officer—*SQUADRON-LEADER SWANSON—*comes in quickly. He is about fifty-five, and wears last-war medals but no wings.*)

SWANSON (*coming down* R.). Teddy—thank the Lord I've found you.

TEDDY. Hullo, Gloria——

SWANSON. Come here, quick. (*Seeing* PATRICIA.) Oh, excuse me——

TEDDY. This is my wife. Squadron-Leader Swanson—our adjutant—a shocking type.

SWANSON. Good evening, Mrs. Graham. Can you spare me your husband for a moment ?

TEDDY. Is it anything important ? We were just——

SWANSON. Yes, it is. Damned important. (*He puts his hat on the counter.*)

(*A pause.* TEDDY *nods.*)

TEDDY. Oh. Oh, I see. (*To* PATRICIA.) You'll have to excuse me, darling. Go along to our room.

(PATRICIA *looks from one to the other. Then without a word, she goes along the passage.*)

SWANSON (*sternly, crossing to the* C. *table*). What's the idea of marrying a glamour girl ? She's far too good-looking for a type like you.

TEDDY (*down to* L. *of the table*). I could marry Garbo if I tried. What's the trouble, Gloria ?

SWANSON. You know.

TEDDY (*simply*). Damn !

SWANSON. Just come through from Group.

TEDDY. What time take off ?

SWANSON. Twenty-two hours. Briefing nineteen-forty-five.

TEDDY. This is a hell of a time to let us know. Who's going ? Everyone ?

SWANSON. No. A apples, L london, U uncle. And a kite from the Polish squadron—S sugar.

TEDDY. Johnny's. What's the job ?

SWANSON. Special. Very hush-hush. Not exactly a piece of cake, I believe. What in hell was the idea of pooping off the station like that ? They told you this morning something might still come through.

TEDDY. They knew where to find me. I went up to ops at five-thirty. There was nothing on then—and, Gawd, if Group can't make up their minds by five-thirty——

SWANSON. I wouldn't have put it past you, P/O Prune, to have gone roaring off to Brighton or somewhere for the week-end, and then we'd have had a pretty little court-martial on our hands.

TEDDY. You'd have got me out of it, Gloria.

SWANSON. I damn well wouldn't. What have you done with your crew ?

TEDDY. They're all up at the station except Miller, the gunner. He's here. His wife's come down, poor blighter. I suppose we can't find a relief for him, can we ?

SWANSON. No, it's too late. I gather you brought old Count Kiss-me-Quick down with you——

TEDDY. Yes. He's here.

SWANSON. Then you'd all better get cracking. You can use my car——

TEDDY. I'll use my own. (*He goes to the foot of the stairs. Calling.*) Johnny ! Sergeant Miller ! (*Turns to* SWANSON.) What's the met. report like ?

SWANSON. All right, I think.

(*The* COUNT *appears, followed by* DORIS.)

COUNT. What is, please ?

TEDDY. Come on down.

(*The* COUNT *comes down to* L. *of the stairs.*)

Sorry, Doris. No wives.

DORIS. Oh. I get you. O.K., ducks.

(*She goes back up the stairs, meeting* DUSTY *on the landing.*)

You're wanted, Dusty.

(*She goes out.* DUSTY *looks down at the group below, then frames an inaudible but obvious expletive.*)

DUSTY (*calling*). Stay there, Maudie. I'll be back in a tic. (*He comes downstairs, between the* COUNT *and* TEDDY.)

TEDDY (*in a low voice*). We've got some nice cheerful news for you boys. It's going to make your evening.

DUSTY. Didn't I tell you this'd happen ?

TEDDY. You did, Dusty.

COUNT. We—go out to-night ?

TEDDY. Yes, Johnny. Take off twenty-two hours. Briefing nineteen-forty-five.

DUSTY. 'Ell of a time to tell us, I must say. Caught us bending proper this time. Group must be fair busting their stays with laughter.

TEDDY. I bet they are. Are you all ready, Johnny ?

COUNT. I go upstairs. One minute only.

(He goes off upstairs.)

TEDDY. Go and say good-bye to your wife, Dusty. I'm sorry this had to happen. I'll drive you both up. I'll just go and get the car out.

SWANSON. I'll follow you later. I'm not going away from here without a drink.

(SWANSON *goes into the lounge.* TEDDY *goes out at the back.* MAUDIE *has come quietly down the stairs.)*

DUSTY *(turns and sees her).* Maudie, I told you to stay in the room.

MAUDIE. What's up, Dave ?

DUSTY. Bit of bad luck, Maudie. I got to leave you to-night.

MAUDIE. I only got one night. Don't go out to-night, Dave.

DUSTY. It's not my doing, old girl. Been a bit of a muck-up at Group.

MAUDIE. What's Group ?

DUSTY. Group headquarters. Where the orders come from.

MAUDIE. Why don't you tell them your wife's come down, and she's only got the one night ?

DUSTY. No go, Maudie.

MAUDIE. Oh, Dave.

DUSTY. I tell you what. After you've had your supper— good supper they give you 'ere too—you go up to bed, see, and get some sleep. I'll be back 'bout four or maybe five, and we'll still have some time together. Your 'bus don't go till one to-morrow——

MAUDIE. All right, Dave. *(She starts upstairs.)* If they tell you you've got to do it, you've got to do it, I suppose. Try and get back soon.

DUSTY. 'Course I will. I'll be back before you know I'm gone. I got the best skipper in England and I'll tell him to step on it to-night.

(TEDDY *has come in quickly in time to hear the last sentence. He waits a second, then walks forward to the banisters.)*

TEDDY. Oh, Mrs. Miller, I'm terribly sorry about this—it's the cruellest bad luck.

MAUDIE (*leaning over the banisters*). I was asking Dave, Mr. Graham, if it wouldn't do no good to tell this Group that his wife's come down——

TEDDY (*gently*). I'm afraid not. You see, there wouldn't be time.

MAUDIE. Oh, I see. (*To* DUSTY.) You going now ?

DUSTY. This minute, Maudie.

MAUDIE. Good-bye, Dave.

DUSTY. Good-bye, old girl. You do what I told you, now. Get some sleep. (*He crosses to the door and picks up his hat.*)

TEDDY. If there's anything you want, Mrs. Miller, I know my wife would be only too glad——

MAUDIE. No, thank you, Mr. Graham. There won't be nothing.

(DUSTY *does the " thumbs-up " sign and she does it too.* DUSTY *goes out quickly.*)

(*On the stairs.*) Take care of him, sir. Don't let him go doing none of those silly tricks like he was telling me about—shooting at searchlights and such.

TEDDY. No, I won't. I promise you.

(MAUDIE *goes out, passing the* COUNT, *who comes running down the stairs.*)

COUNT (*crossing to the hat-stand*). I am most happy. It is two weeks we have not go out.

TEDDY (*gets his coat off the stand and puts it on*). You're a glutton for trouble, aren't you ?

COUNT. Please ?

TEDDY. Doesn't matter. Jump in the car, Johnny. I'll follow you. (*As the* COUNT *goes out.*) TEDDY (*crosses to the banisters and calls*). Pat !

(PATRICIA *appears on the landing.*)

PATRICIA (*descending the stairs*). You're going up to the station, aren't you ?

TEDDY (*down to her at the foot of the stairs*). Yes. I've got to rush. I just want to say good-bye. I hoped this wasn't going to happen while you were here. I'm awfully sorry.

PATRICIA. It's a raid, I suppose.

TEDDY. It's not exactly a practice stooge-around.

PATRICIA (*helplessly*). Teddy, I don't know what to say.

TEDDY. Happy landing—or just—come back——

PATRICIA. Come back.

(TEDDY *kisses her.*)

TEDDY. Good-bye, darling. God willing, I'll be waking you up at the hellish hour of five or so to-morrow morning. Oh, by the way, whatever it was you had to tell me will have to wait till I get back   I suppose that's all right with you ?

PATRICIA. Yes. That's all right with me.

(TEDDY *goes abruptly to the door up* R. *and turns. He smiles at* PATRICIA *and goes out.* MAUDIE *comes down and sits in the armchair above the fire.* DORIS *follows. She passes* PATRICIA *and pats her arm comfortingly, without saying anything.*)

(*Effects Cue No.* 12 : *Car door slam.*)

(MRS. OAKES *enters from the office behind the counter, and goes up to draw the curtains.*)

(*Effects Cue No.* 13 : *The sound of a car moving away breaks the silence.*)

CURTAIN.

ACT II

Scene 1

SCENE.—*The same, about three hours later.*

PETER *is sitting on the fender, and* PATRICIA *is sitting above the fire.* MAUDIE *is in a chair* R., *apart from them. Coffee things are on the table* R. *The wireless is going.*

(*Effects Cue No.* 1 : *B.B.C. announcement.*)

ANNOUNCER.   —at the controlled price of two shillings and tenpence a pound, and will shortly be obtainable throughout the United Kingdom. (*A pause.*) That is the end of the nine o'clock news.

PATRICIA. Turn it off.

ANNOUNCER. To-night's talk is . . .

(PETER *turns off the radio.*)

(*Effects : Radio off.*)

PATRICIA. You don't mind, do you, Mrs. Miller ?

MAUDIE. No, thank you. I wasn't listening anyway.

(*The lounge door* R. *opens and* DORIS *appears accompanied by a rattle and hum of voices. She has a drink in her hand, and a set of darts.*)

DORIS. Anyone hear the nine o'clock ? I clean forgot the time. (*Going up to the counter and taking a cigarette out of her bag.*)

(PETER *rises.*)

PATRICIA. We've just turned it off.

DORIS. There wasn't anything fresh, I suppose. No pincers on anything anywhere ?

" WIGGY " JONES (CORPORAL *appears at the bar door.*)

WIGGY JONES. Come on, Countess. We still want a double two.

DORIS (*to* WIGGY). Take my turn, Wig.

(WIGGY *shuts the door and the noise stops.*)

Why don't you all come in here ? We're having a slap-up do. (*To* R.C.)

PATRICIA. I don't think so, if you don't mind.

DORIS. Perhaps you're right. The boys are a bit noisy.

PATRICIA (*hastily*). It's not that——

DORIS (*sitting on the* R. *arm of the sofa*). I know, ducks. You
don't have to tell me. Do you remember the old joke about
wives waiting up for their husbands at five in the morning with
a rolling-pin ? Makes me laugh sometimes when I think of it,
it does, really. (*Rising.*) There's a full moon to-night. I think
I'll just go and have a look.

(*She disappears to the outside door, up* R., *and closes it.*)

PETER. I've rather taken to the Countess. What's going to
happen to her after the war, I wonder ?

PATRICIA. Oh, she'll go to Poland with her Johnny, and find
herself mistress of an enormous estate, with thousands of serfs
or moujiks or whatever they are. She'll probably make a big
success of it.

PETER. Supposing there is an after the war.

PATRICIA. Or supposing there's a Johnny.

(DORIS *re-enters and stands by inside the door.*)

PETER (*slowly*). Or supposing he wants to take her.

PATRICIA. Yes, that's rather a point, I admit.

PETER. I'm afraid it's *the* point. Our Countess has a personal
interest in the war continuing.

DORIS (*drawing the curtain over the inside door*). The sireens
have just gone in Skillingworth.

(WIGGY *reappears at the bar door. Bar noises are heard off.*)

WIGGY. What's yours, Countess ?

DORIS (*over her shoulder*). Gin and ginger.

(WIGGY *exits, shutting the door.*)

(*To* PATRICIA.) It's on Hull, I believe, but they may drop a
couple on the aerodrome. They do sometimes. Tinkerty tonk,
Mrs. Miller.

MAUDIE. Tinkerty tonk !

(DORIS *disappears into the bar.*)

(*Effects Cue No. 2 : German bomber in the distance.*)

PETER. Purely as a matter of idle interest—is there a shelter
here ?

PATRICIA. I don't know. If there is, I don't suppose anyone
would bother to use it.

PETER. I suppose if I'd been in England longer than a mere
three months, I might become as blasé about raids as you are.
(*Sharply.*) Listen. Those ours ?

MAUDIE (*breaking a long pause*). Theirs.

PETER. Oh, are they ? How do you know ?

MAUDIE. I lived in London till we were bombed out.

PATRICIA. I live in London too, but I can never tell the difference.

MAUDIE. Perhaps you don't listen for it, like what I do.

PETER. Bombs ?

(*Effects Cue No.* 3 : *Distant gunfire. German bomber fades.*)

PATRICIA (*smiling*). No—guns. You've got a lot to learn.

PETER. Superior beast.

(*He touches her hand and both look round at* MAUDIE.)

PATRICIA (*she gets up, puts her coffee cup on* c. *table and goes over to* MAUDIE). Is there anything you'd like, Mrs. Miller ? Some coffee or something ?

(MAUDIE *looks up.*)

MAUDIE. No, thank you, Mrs. Graham.

PATRICIA. That's not a very comfortable chair you've chosen. Wouldn't you like to come over by the fire ?

MAUDIE. I'm quite comfy here, thank you.

PATRICIA. It's rotten luck, your having only the one night.

MAUDIE. I'll have a bit of to-morrow, before the 'bus goes.

PETER (*coming* c. *behind* PATRICIA). Do you have to go far ?

MAUDIE. Only to St. Albans.

PATRICIA. Can't you possibly stay another night ?

MAUDIE. No, I must be to work seven o'clock Monday. It's a laundry, you see.

PETER. Couldn't you ring your people up and explain ? I'll ring them up for you, if you like.

MAUDIE. Oh no, please. You mustn't.

PETER. Why not ?

MAUDIE. They wouldn't like it. I'd be losing my job, and that'd never do—not now it wouldn't. Besides, I must be to work Monday morning. There's a lot to be done Mondays.

PATRICIA. I'm sure if you'd let Mr. Kyle explain——

MAUDIE (*firmly*). No, Mrs. Graham. Thank you all the same.

(*A pause.*)

PETER. How do you like your work in the laundry, Mrs. Miller ?

MAUDIE. Oh, it's not so bad. I'm new to it, of course.

PETER. You haven't always done that kind of work ?

MAUDIE. Oh no. Not peace time, I didn't. I didn't have to work peace time. Dave had a good job, you see, and we had our own home in Eccleston Bridge Road—nice place it was. Of course it's down now. Dave worked in London Transport—conductor—might have been inspector quite soon——

PATRICIA. And now he's a rear gunner in a Wellington bomber, shooting down Messerschmitts. (*To* MAUDIE.) Don't you ever find it unreal, what's happened to your husband and yourself ?

MAUDIE. Unreal ? No, I don't see it's unreal. It's happened, hasn't it ?

(PATRICIA *nods*.)

Mind you, I'm not saying I like him being a gunner, it's not good for him in those turret things. They're wickedly cold. He told me so himself—and he gets horrible backaches. He used to get them when he was working on the 'buses. Besides it's no good saying they always get back from these raids, because they don't—not all of them. Then I'm not saying I liked being bombed out and going to live in St. Albans with Dave's Aunt Ella, who I've never got on with and never will—and working at the Snowflake—but what I say is, there's a war on, and things have got to be a bit different, and we've just got to get used to it—that's all.

PETER. Yes, I see. Very sensible.

(*There is a sudden burst of voices as the lounge door opens and* DORIS *comes in. From the lounge we can hear the barman's voice shouting* : " Time, gentlemen, please. It's gone half-past nine. Time, gentlemen, please." PETER *crosses to the fire and* PATRICIA *sits on the sofa*.)

DORIS (*humming to herself*). I don't want to join the Air Force
                I don't want to go to war—
Phew ! The Countess Skriczevinsky is a teeny bit tippy-o. (*Seeing* MAUDIE.) Hullo, Mrs. Miller, dear. Everything okay ?

MAUDIE (*with dignity*). Yes, thank you for asking.

DORIS. Nothing you'd like me to get you ? A little dinky, or anything ?

MAUDIE (*cuttingly*). It's very kind of you, I'm sure, but I won't have a little—dinky. (*She sniffs contemptuously and gets up from her chair and crosses to the stairs*.) Good night, Mrs. Graham.

(DORIS *moves up and leans on the counter*.)

PATRICIA. Good night, Mrs. Miller.

MAUDIE. Good night, Mr. Kyle.

PETER. Good night.

MAUDIE (*moving down to* PATRICIA *again*). Oh, by the way, Mrs. Graham, on account of my Dave is rather funny about me not mentioning his backaches to nobody, please don't say nothing to him about me having told you about them.

PATRICIA. All right, Mrs. Miller. I won't say a word.

(MAUDIE *starts up the stairs*.)

DORIS (*calling*). Good night, Mrs. Miller, ducks. Sleep tight.

MAUDIE. I'd say you were more likely to do that than what I am, Countess.

(*She goes out.*)

DORIS (*laughing*). Oo, did you hear that ? I bought that properly, didn't I ? Sleep tight ! I'll give her sleep tight !

PATRICIA. I shouldn't brood on it, Doris.

DORIS (*down* R.C.). I suppose she thinks it's common for a Countess to have a few drinks with the boys.

PETER. As a matter of fact, I know lots of Countesses who don't stop at having a few drinks with the boys.

(DORIS *turns slowly in his direction. She glares at him.*)

DORIS. Now you're making fun of me, Mr. Peter Kyle, and I don't like it.

PETER (*contrite*). I'm sorry.

DORIS. Now don't blame me for being a Countess. It's not my fault. I didn't want it. I'd much rather be plain Mrs.—but Johnny likes people to call me Countess, so I've got to let them, see. But don't you be funny about me just because of that.

PATRICIA (*hastily*). He wasn't being funny about you, Doris.

PETER. Of course I wasn't——

DORIS (*putting her glass on the table* R.). I overheard everything you said about me and my Johnny just now. How I had a personal interest in the war going on.

(PETER *and* PATRICIA *start.*)

PETER. I think you misheard me.

DORIS. Misheard my eye. That's what you said all right.

PETER. If I did, I've no idea what I meant——

DORIS. I know what you meant. You meant my Johnny's going to leave me flat the minute the war's over. That's what you meant. I'm only all right for him as long as the war goes on, and as soon as it's over and he gets back home, he'll realize he's made an awful muck-up in marrying me and he'll—he'll——

(*She chokes and turns her back quickly.* PATRICIA *rises and goes down to her.*)

PATRICIA. Doris, my dear, don't be so idiotic. Even if Mr. Kyle did say that—and he didn't—it doesn't matter because you know perfectly well it isn't true.

DORIS. I don't know it isn't true. I wish I did. I think it *is* true. (*To behind the sofa.*) But I don't want the war to go on—just because of that——

PETER (*up to the foot of the stairs*). I never said you did.

(*A pause.*)

DORIS. Oh dear. I've gone and made a fool of myself again.
Sorry, dear. Sorry, Mr. Kyle. Oh dear—Peter Kyle! I've
been longing to meet him all my life! Then, when I do, I go
and snap his head off.

PETER (*crossing to her*). I really *am* most terribly sorry if I
said anything to make you think——

DORIS. Oh, for heaven's sake! I'd no business to listen,
anyway. Forget it. Wonder if it's clouding over at all. (*She
goes to the window.*) Turn out the light for a sec. will you, ducks?

(*Lighting Cue No. 1: Lights off.*)

(PETER *turns the light out from below the fire.* DORIS *sticks her
head out of the window.*)

No, it's a lovely night, I'm afraid.

(PATRICIA *crosses up to the window* R. *of* DORIS.)

PATRICIA. Why afraid?

DORIS. If the weather was dud they might call it off. They
won't, though. There's a lovely moon. What's the time?

PETER. A quarter to ten.

DORIS. They haven't lit the flare path yet.

PATRICIA. What's the flare path?

DORIS. Lights in a line—so that they can see when they're
taking off. You ought to know that, married to a flight-loot.

(MRS. OAKES *comes in from the bar and turns on the light.*)

(*Lighting Cue No. 2: Lights on.*)

MRS. OAKES (*with a scream*). My black-out! (*She turns off
the lights again.*)

(*Lighting Cue No. 3: Lights off.*)

DORIS. All right. We'll do it, Mrs. Oakes.

(*They draw the curtains.* PATRICIA *sits on the window-seat.*
DORIS *sits on the chair* L. *of the door.*)

Will you put the lights on, Mr. Kyle?

(PETER *does so.*)

(*Lighting Cue No. 4: Lights on.*)

MRS. OAKES (*up to* DORIS). Have they gone yet?

DORIS. You shouldn't know they were going at all.

MRS. OAKES. Well, something made them all go back to the
aerodrome in an awful hurry. (*With a heavy wink.*) I suppose
it could have been an E.N.S.A. show. (*Crossing to the foot of the
stairs.*) What time are they going to be back? That's all that
concerns me.

DORIS (*returning the wink*). My guess is the E.N.S.A. show will be over about five in the morning.

MRS. OAKES. Your guess is as good as anyone's, Countess. Will the last one up please turn off the lights ? I'm going to bed. Breakfast is at eight-thirty, Mr. Kyle—to-morrow being Sunday we don't serve it in the bedrooms, as we are so shockingly under-staffed.

PETER. That's quite all right. I don't have breakfast.

(MRS. OAKES, *on her way up the stairs, stops dead.*)

MRS. OAKES (*appalled*). You don't have breakfast ?

PETER (*nervously*). No. I—er—just a cup of tea.

DORIS. He's an actor, you see, Mrs. Oakes. He has to keep his figure.

MRS. OAKES. His figure, I see. I'm afraid I can make no reduction in the price of the room.

PETER. That's quite all right——

MRS. OAKES (*severely*). It's not all right at all, Mr. Kyle. I'm sure I don't like to charge people for what they don't have. But, you see, there *is* a war on, and if you don't have breakfast you must just take the consequences, that's all. Good night.

(*She goes out.*)

PETER. What consequences ? Duodenal ulcer ?

PATRICIA (*rising, comes behind the sofa, laughing*). No. darling. Paying for it.

(*There is a slightly awkward moment following this slip.*)

DORIS (*rising, comes down* R.). Wonderful the way you stage people darling each other. To hear you sometimes, you'd think you were passionately in love. (*Suddenly.*) There's the All Clear—can you hear it ?

PATRICIA (*after listening*). Yes, I can—just. Good.

DORIS (*almost simultaneously*). Damn ! (*Answering* PATRICIA's *unspoken inquiry.*) They wouldn't take off with Jerry over-head. They couldn't light the flare path, you see. (*She sits on the* R. *arm of the sofa.*) Of course sometimes old Jerry hangs about over the aerodrome for hours, and they don't know he's there. Then, just when they've lit the flare path and the boys are taking off—or coming in more likely—he'll swoop down on them and shoot them up. You're a sitting target when you're coming in—so Teddy says—and you're dead beat probably and thanking God you've got back and then suddenly—— (*She stops.*) Filthy trick, I think. Of course, we do the same over on their aerodromes. What's the time, Mr. Kyle ? Sorry to keep troubling you.

PETER. Ten minutes to ten.

DORIS (*crossing to the counter and picking up her bag*). I'll go and watch the take-off from my room. You see better from up there. It won't be for a bit yet, of course. Good night. (*She crosses behind the sofa to the stairs.*)

PATRICIA. Good night.

DORIS (*to* PETER). Sorry, ducks.

PETER (*imploringly*). Please!

DORIS (*laughing*). Please! You sound like my Johnny. (*On the stairs.*) If there's anything you want in the middle of the night, Pat dearie, can't sleep, or anything—don't worry about waking me up. I'll be quite glad to have company. Nighty-night.

(*She goes out. There is a silence between* PETER *and* PATRICIA *for a moment.*)

PETER (*with a sudden explosion*). God damn it.

(PATRICIA *goes to him, but says nothing.*)

What right has she to go listening at doors? It wouldn't have been so bad if she didn't know it was true.

(PATRICIA *puts her hand out and touches his. He takes it and looks down at it, examining a ring on her finger.*)

I had rather good taste for a film star in those days, hadn't I?

PATRICIA. It was very good taste. I suppose I should have sent it back to you. That's what a nice girl would have done.

PETER. A nice girl wouldn't have had anything to do with me in the first place.

PATRICIA. Oh, I think she would, Pete. (*As an afterthought.*) Not that I'm claiming to be a nice girl.

PETER. You're the nicest girl I've ever known or ever shall know. (*Moving to centre table.*) Pat, don't bully me if I say something to you, will you?

PATRICIA. No, darling. (*She sits in the armchair above the fire.*)

PETER. Well—I'm getting old, Pat.

PATRICIA. Old? You're thirty-nine.

PETER. Thirty-nine when you left me, forty-one now. Not old, really, just a nice, ripe, fruity middle-age. Perfectly all right if I were a good enough actor to play middle-aged parts.

PATRICIA. But you are.

PETER. The Studio doesn't think so. After my next picture I'm out. Oh, well, it's not only that, Pat, and this will sound— (*he smiles at her shamefacedly*) funny, I suppose, if you happen to look at it like that. (*He sits on the* L. *arm of the sofa.*) It's the war, you see. I don't understand it, Pat—you know that— democracy—freedom—rights of men—I can talk quite glibly about them, but they don't mean anything, not to me. All I know is that my own little private world is going—well, it's gone

really—and the rest of the world—the real world—has turned
its back on me and left me out and though I want to get into the
circle, I can't. (*He rises and stands facing the* o. *table.*) I hate
that, Pat—I hate being left out in the cold. I know it's a selfish
way of looking at it, but I don't care. So you see—I do—what
with one thing and another—I do happen to need you—— (*His
voice trails away into an embarrassed silence.*)

(PATRICIA *crosses to* L. *of* PETER.)

PATRICIA (*uncertainly*). Yes, you do, Pete. I'm glad that
you do. That's what I've always loved about you, that you
needed me. Even when I first met you I wasn't taken in by that
self-assured act of yours, because I could see what was under-
neath and I loved it because it was simple and childish and I
don't know—sort 'of helpless.

PETER. Thank you, Pat. All very shy-making. It's only
that I worry sometimes.

PATRICIA. You don't need to. You should know that by
now.

PETER. Things can happen.

PATRICIA. Not to me.

PETER (*lightly*). You're a faithful type ?

(PATRICIA *winces slightly.*)

(*Quickly.*) I'm sorry.

PATRICIA (*returning to the fire*). It's all right. It's only that
I'd forgotten him for the moment.

(*There is a noise at the front door.* SWANSON *comes in, carrying a
rug.*)

SWANSON (*jovially*). Hullo—'ullo. Mrs. Graham, eh ?
Thought I'd find you up. (*He looks at* PETER.)

PATRICIA. Good evening, Squadron-Leader. This is Peter
Kyle—Squadron-Leader Swanson. (*She sits below the fire.*)

SWANSON (*down to the sofa*). Oh yes. You're the actor type,
aren't you ? (*He puts the rug on the* R. *arm of the sofa.*) I
heard all about you from Teddy. He's been burbling about
meeting you, all the evening. Shooting a terrific line. (PETER
smiles politely.) I say, I suppose you wouldn't like to come up to
the station to-morrow ? Say a few words or something. Give
the blokes a hell of a thrill—something to write to their girl
friends about, instead of official secrets.

PETER (*sits on the* L. *arm of the sofa*). I'd love to, but as a
matter of fact, I'm leaving for London to-morrow. (*He lights a
cigarette.*)

SWANSON (*hangs up his coat*). Oh, pity. Well, perhaps some
other time. Waiting up for the take-off, eh ? Won't be long

now. After they've gone take my advice—toddle off to bed and get some sleep. Won't seem any time before he's back again. As a matter of fact, old Teddy asked me to come along and see if you were all right and all that.

PATRICIA. It's very kind of you.

SWANSON (*returning to the sofa*). Not at all. (*Apologetically.*) As a matter of fact I'm not much good as a comforter on these occasions. I get so damned nervous myself.

PETER (*making conversation*). You're not flying to-night yourself ?

SWANSON. Good Lord—I don't fly. Look. Nothing up here. (*He flicks his breast.*) Just an old wingless wonder. Adjutant. (*He picks up the rug and crosses to the chair above the fire.*) Combination nurse and maid of all work to the station. No business in the Air Force at all, really. Ought to be in the Army like I was in the last war. My bed for to-night. (*He puts the rug on the chair.*)

PETER. My God ! It isn't *your* room I've taken, is it ?

SWANSON. Lord, no. I sleep up at the station as a rule. But when the boys are out on a job, I like to be up when they come in, and I can't trust that damn fool of a batman to wake me. It's warmer down here, too.

PATRICIA. It's not an awfully good fire. (*She rises and arranges the cushions and rug.*)

SWANSON. It'll burn up. Teddy calls me Gloria, you know. No respect for senior rank. Shocking. (*He starts to put some logs on the fire.*)

PETER. Mrs. Graham. Are you going to take the Squadron-Leader's advice, or are you going to wait up ? If you are, I'd be very happy to——

PATRICIA. I'll go to bed. I think it's better.

PETER. I see. Well, good night.

PATRICIA. Good night. (*She comes to the fire and pokes it, kneeling below* SWANSON.)

PETER (*on the stairs*). Good night, sir.

(SWANSON, *who has been blowing away at the fire, straightens himself.*)

SWANSON. What's that ? Oh, are you off to bed ? Good-night. Oh, I say.

PETER. Yes ?

SWANSON. Have you met Alice Faye ?

PETER. Yes. Once.

SWANSON. Good Lord ! (*He returns to the fire.*)

PETER. Good night.

(*He goes out.* PATRICIA *is still kneeling beside* SWANSON *who is puffing away at the fire without effect.*)

PATRICIA. You'll never get it to go like that. Here, let me.
(*She takes a sheet of newspaper and uses it to draw the fire.*)
SWANSON. Takes a woman to think of that.

(*He looks at his watch. A pause. The fire burns up.*)

PATRICIA. You're very fond of Teddy, Squadron-Leader ?
SWANSON. Who isn't ? Look out. That'll burn. (*He pulls
the paper away.*)

(*The fire is glowing.*)

PATRICIA. Who isn't ? (*She sits on the fender.*)
SWANSON (*rises*). Of course, I'm fond of 'em all, if it comes to
that, but I don't know the others as well as I know old P/O
Prune. We call him that, you know.
PATRICIA. Yes. He told me.
SWANSON. He's not quite so prunish as he lets on. I've seen
him sometimes—— (*He breaks off.*) Dammit, you're his wife.
You must know him better than I do. (*He sits on the arm of
the chair above the fire.*)
PATRICIA. Yes, of course.
SWANSON. I hate all this patriotic bilge in the newspapers,
but, my God, we do owe these boys something, you know.
PATRICIA. Yes. (*She crosses to the sofa and sits on the L. arm.*)
SWANSON (*rises*). It's going pretty well, now. Thanks to
you. You've been married a year or so now, haven't you ?
PATRICIA. Just under a year.
SWANSON. He's damned lucky, if I may say so. I was scared
stiff when I heard he'd married an actress. He's just the type
who might have fallen for some awful bottle-party floosie who'd
have let him down with a wallop. (*He fumbles in his pocket and
produces a slip of paper.*) Oh, by the way, I knew I had something to show you. Some joker put this in the Mess Suggestion
Book. I copied it out. Thought it might amuse you. (*He
hands it to her.*) Read it out.
PATRICIA. " Suggested that Flight-Lieutenant Graham shall
in future be permitted to mention his wife's name not more
than ten times per diem ; and that on each subsequent mention
of the said wife's said name—to wit, Patricia, or Pat, Paddy,
Paddykins and other such nauseating diminutives—over and
above the allotted ten times per diem, Flight-Lieutenant Graham
shall forfeit to all officers within hearing a pint of beer."

(*She finishes reading.* SWANSON *chuckles delightedly.* PATRICIA
continues staring at the slip of paper.)

SWANSON. You see. Practically everyone in the mess has
signed it—even little Tinker Bell, the Signals Officer—who dies
of fright if you speak to him.

(PATRICIA *hands it back.*)

No, you keep it. I thought it might be fun for you to have —with all the names on it——

(*Effects Cue No. 4 : Take-off—crash record ready.*)

(*An aircraft's engines can be heard.* SWANSON *turns abruptly to the window.*)

Turn off the light.

(*Lighting Cue No. 5 : Lights off.*)

(PATRICIA *turns out the lights from the switch below the fire.* SWAN-SON *pulls back the curtains, allowing the moonlight to illumine the room.* PATRICIA *joins him at the window.*)

There's the flare path—do you see ? Those little points of light. There's one taking off now.

(*The noise of the aircraft's engines increases.*)

There's one off, thank God !

(*The noise passes directly overhead and fades.*)

It's a hellish tricky business taking off on a night like this, with no wind and a full load of bombs. Hellish tricky. Worse than landing.

(*Fade in aircraft.*)

Here's the next just starting his run.

PATRICIA. Which is Teddy's ?

SWANSON. Can't tell. They don't take off in any particular order. There are only four aircraft flying to-night—A Apple, L London, U Uncle—that's Teddy, and S Sugar from the Polish Squadron. (*Sharply.*) God !

PATRICIA. What's the matter ?

SWANSON. It's all right. He's off. I thought he wasn't going to make it. He must have cleared that fence by inches.

(*The noise passes overhead and fades.*)

Next one's coming up. (*Sharply.*) Hullo ! What's that ? The first one seems to be circling round up there. Can you hear him ?

PATRICIA. No. Do you think it might be a German ?

SWANSON. I hope to God it's not. There is one circling round up there. Ah, there he goes, the next one—do you see ? That dark shape——

PATRICIA (*in alarm*). His engines are on fire.

SWANSON (*laughing*). No. That's the exhaust. It always looks like that. You can see it miles away. Useful to night fighters. Good boy ! Nice take-off. One more to go. (*He listens intently again.*) Ah, here he comes. See him ?

PATRICIA. Yes, I see him.

SWANSON. God!

PATRICIA (*almost simultaneously*). Why have they turned out the flare path ?

(*Effects Cue No. 5 : Machine gun and four bombs.*)

(*There is a sudden rattle of machine-gun fire, followed by four loud but dull sounding explosions.*)

They're bombing the aerodrome. It was a German.

SWANSON (*shouting*). Brakes, you idiot, brakes ! Don't take off.

(DORIS *runs down the stairs and stands at the foot.*)

(*Effects Cue No. 6.*)

(*There is another rattle of machine-gun fire, followed by another explosion sharper than the bomb bursts and with a tearing, rending sound, following it. PATRICIA stifles a scream. A dull red glow appears at the window. SWANSON pulls the curtains to violently.*)

(*Quietly.*) Put the lights on. (*He goes out of the front door.*)

PATRICIA (*crossing to the counter, in a panic*). I can't find the switch. I can't find the switch. I can't . . .

DORIS (*in matter-of-fact tones*). It's on the left of the door, over the bell.

(*Lighting Cue No. 6 : Lights on.*)

(*The room is suddenly flooded with light. PATRICIA is standing by the switch. DORIS is at R. of the foot of the stairs, fully dressed. She is standing quite still. SWANSON re-enters and goes to the telephone on the counter and lifts the receiver.*)

SWANSON. Milchester two-three.

(PETER *appears fully dressed. He runs downstairs.*)

PETER. What happened ?

SWANSON. An aircraft crashed or was shot down, taking off.

(PETER *walks across to* PATRICIA. MAUDIE *has come down the stairs behind him in time to hear* SWANSON'S *last line.*)

MAUDIE (*coming downstairs*). It's not Dave, is it ?

DORIS (*puts her hand on* MAUDIE'S *arm and stops her*). We don't know who it is, dear. The Squadron-Leader's finding out for us.

SWANSON (*at the telephone*). Hullo. Put me through to Controller—Squadron-Leader Swanson . . . Hullo, Manning ! Swanson here . . . Yes, I saw it. What happened ? . . . No,

no, of course not, but at least you know which aircraft it was.
. . . Yes . . . I see . . . all right. (*He rings off and turns round.*) The crashed aircraft is A Apples.

MAUDIE. Dave.

DORIS. No, dear. We're all right.

SWANSON. L London U Uncle—that's Teddy's—

(PETER *puts his hand on* PATRICIA'S *shoulder.*)

—and S Sugar are all airborne, and are now on their way——

(*There is a pause. Nobody moves.* SWANSON *turns abruptly and goes out.*)

CURTAIN.

NOTE.—While the CURTAIN *is lowered, denoting the passing of time, the sound of an aircraft's engines in flight should continue to be audible until some seconds after the raising of the* CURTAIN *on Scene 2.*

SCENE 2

SCENE.—*The same, about 5.30 a.m. the following morning.*

The sound of an aircraft's engines can be heard. SWANSON *and* DORIS *are at the window, outlined against the faint light of early dawn. The sound of the engines ceases, as they are throttled back.*

(*Effects Cue No.* 1 : *Bomber landing and taxi-ing back.*)

SWANSON (*at length*). He's down all right.

DORIS. It's Johnny's, I'm almost sure. I recognized the engines.

(*The noise of the plane taxi-ing back is heard faintly.*)

SWANSON. That's absurd, my dear Countess, if you don't mind my saying so. All Wellingtons sound alike.

DORIS. Not to me they don't.

(PATRICIA *appears on the stairs in her dressing-gown.*)

PATRICIA. Is that one of them back ?

SWANSON. 'Morning, Mrs. Graham. Yes, it's the second to come in. The first one landed about twenty minutes ago.

PATRICIA (*coming down to* L. *of the sofa*). I must have been asleep. (*She lights a cigarette.*) Is either of them Teddy's ?

(*Effects Cue No.* 2 : *Taxi-ing back fades.*)

SWANSON. Don't know yet. Don't like to keep on ringing Ops.

DORIS (*cheerfully*). We'll know soon enough, anyway.

(MRS. OAKES *comes out of the coffee-room with a loaded tray and cloth. She is in a rather elaborate déshabille.*)

MRS. OAKES (*putting the tray on a chair by the coffee-room door*). May I have the curtains drawn, please ?   I want to switch on the lights.

(DORIS *goes down to the switch by the bar.*)

SWANSON.   It's still black-out, I suppose.

(*Lighting Cue No.* 1 : *Lights on in room.*)

(*He pulls the curtains to, blacking out the room, as* DORIS *switches on the lights, and then clears a cup and ashtray off the* C. *table on to the table* R.)

MRS. OAKES.   It's black-out until five fifty-two.   (*She indicates the* C. *table.*)   Will you give me a hand with this table ? (*She brings the table from* R. *of the stairs down* L. *in front of the fire.*)

SWANSON.   Of course.   What's the time now ?

(DORIS *and* SWANSON *put the* C. *table with the one at the fire.*)

MRS. OAKES.   Just gone half-past.   I thought I'd lay a table in here.   It's warmer with that fire.   (*She lays the cloth.   Acidly.*) I must say, I can't quite understand how it has kept in all this time.   I usually have to relight it.

(DORIS *has gone up for the tray and brings it down to the table.*)

SWANSON (*embarrassed*).   Well, as a matter of fact——
MRS. OAKES.   Quite, Squadron-Leader.

(*She and* DORIS *lay the table as* SWANSON *crosses to the sofa.*)

I see.   (*To* PATRICIA.)   Shall I lay a place for you, Mrs. Graham ? I expect you'll want to have breakfast with your husband, won't you—now that you're up ?

(PATRICIA *has been walking restlessly round the room.*)

NOTE.—Lighting Cue No. 2 : *Bring up exterior lighting ready for drawn window curtains and Cue No.* 3 *at the end of the Act.*

PATRICIA (*down* R.).   I won't want much to eat.
MRS. OAKES.   There isn't much to eat.   Now let me see— Flight-Lieutenant Graham, Flying Officer Count Skriczevinsky, Sergeant Miller—that'll be five with you, Countess.   I'm afraid I can't provide for casuals like you, Squadron-Leader.

(DORIS *finishes laying the table and crosses to the sofa and sits.*)

SWANSON.   That's all right.   I'm going home anyway as soon as they come.   (*He sits on the* L. *arm of the sofa and takes a cigarette for himself and gives* DORIS *one.*)

Mrs. Oakes (*picking up the tray*).　I won't wake Mrs. Miller up.　I peeped into her room as I came past and she was sound asleep.

Patricia.　Can I help you ?　(*She crosses to the table.*)

Mrs. Oakes.　No, thank you, Mrs. Graham.　(*She starts for the coffee-room door.*)　I can manage very well.

Patricia.　Do you always do this yourself ?

Mrs. Oakes (*at the door*).　Well, I haven't got five hundred servants, Mrs. Graham, and the ones I have got wouldn't stay long if I made them work at this time in the morning.

(*She goes out into the coffee-room.*)

Patricia.　There's one more to come in yet, isn't there ?

Doris.　Yes, ducky.

(Patricia *looks down at the neatly laid table.*)

Patricia.　Five places !　How horribly smug and complacent it looks.

Doris (*soothingly*).　After flying all night they've got to have something to eat when they come back.

Patricia.　Supposing they don't come back ?　(*She crosses* R.)

(*A pause.*)

Doris.　Poor duckie.　This is the first time you've been here for a do, isn't it ?

Patricia (*up* R.).　A do.　Oh God, how I hate all this polite Air Force understatement.　Isn't there a more dignified word for it than a do ?

Swanson (*rising and crossing to the fire*).　Come and sit over here, Mrs. Graham.　Quite a good fire, you know—thanks to me.

(Patricia *looks from* Doris *to* Swanson.)

Patricia.　I think I will.　(*She sits below the fire.*)　I'm sorry. I didn't sleep much.　(*She looks at* Doris *who is fully dressed.*) You didn't sleep at all—either of you.

Doris.　Oh, I went off now and then.　Didn't I, Squadron-Leader ?

Swanson (*crossing to the sofa*).　You snored once.

Doris.　Oh, I didn't.　You fibber !　(*She giggles.*)　I'm sure I don't know what my Johnny would say—the Squadron-Leader and me down here alone together all night and no chaperon.

Swanson.　Probably challenge me to a duel or something. Rapiers at dawn behind the Admin. Block.

Doris.　Serve you right for smirching my honour.　Snored ! I never snored in my life.

Patricia (*staring at* Doris).　I wish I understood.　(*She stops.*)　You're very brave.

(*Effects Cue No. 3 : Car pulling up.　Door slam.　Driving away.*)

D

(*There is the sound of a car in the road outside.* PATRICIA *and* SWANSON *rise abruptly and face the front door. The car draws up outside the hotel. A door bangs and the car moves on. There is a pause. Then* DUSTY *enters. He wears Air Force battle-dress and a high-necked jumper. He puts his hat on the hat-rack.*)

DUSTY. 'Morning, all. (*He makes the " thumbs-up " sign.*)
PATRICIA (*crossing behind the sofa. Quickly*). Teddy——?
DUSTY. Putting the car away, mum. (*Seeing the fire.*) Cor ! Give me a piece of that. (*He walks to the fire, passing* SWANSON *on the way.*) 'Morning, sir.
SWANSON. 'Morning, Sergeant. Good trip ?
DUSTY (*gloomily*). Proper muck-up from beginning to end.
DORIS. S Sugar back yet ?
DUSTY. Not yet, Countess.
SWANSON. You and L London are back, then. You were the first to land, I suppose ?
DUSTY. Yes, sir. (*He lights a cigarette.*) About half an hour ago. (*Exclamatorily.*) What about A Apples ? Shook us considerable, that did.
SWANSON. You saw the crash ?
DUSTY. Yes, I was in the tail, you see, sir. I called up the Skipper and we circled round her for a bit. Cor ! what a blaze. Nobody got out, did they, sir ?
SWANSON (*shortly*). One man was thrown clear. The navigator.
DUSTY. Old Ginger Walsh, that is. Good old Ginger ! Is he hurt bad ?
SWANSON. They think he'll recover.
DUSTY. I'll trot along and see him to-morrow. How's the wife been behaving herself, Countess ? Okay ?
DORIS. Okay, Dusty. She went up to bed early and she's still asleep.
DUSTY. This fire don't half feel good on my behind.

(TEDDY *enters. His wrist has been bound up with a handkerchief. He is similarly dressed to* DUSTY. *He hangs up his hat and coat.*)

SWANSON (*crosses to him at the door*). Hullo, Prune. Trust you to get down first. What did you do—drop your bombs on Bognor and dash for home ?
TEDDY. That's about it—only it wasn't Bognor, it was Littlehampton—wasn't it, Sarge ?
DUSTY. That's right, sir. All our bombs fell in the target area.
TEDDY (*crosses to* PATRICIA, *kisses her*). Hullo, darling.
PATRICIA. Hullo, Teddy.

TEDDY. You shouldn't have got up.

SWANSON (*coming down to* R. *of* TEDDY). What have you done to your wrist, Teddy ?

TEDDY. What ? Oh, that. It's nothing at all. It got into the way of a flame float I was throwing out.

SWANSON. Let's have a look. (*He looks under the handkerchief.*) You ought to have it seen to.

TEDDY (*crosses to the fire*). I'll take it along to the M.O. to-morrow. Hullo, Doris.

DORIS. Hullo, Ted.

SWANSON. What sort of a trip did you have ? Sergeant's just said it was a proper muck-up.

TEDDY (*sits on the fender below* DUSTY). He's prejudiced. I wouldn't let him shoot up a train he'd taken a dislike to.

DUSTY (*gives* TEDDY *a cigarette, who lights it*). It looked so blooming pleased with itself, puffing along down there.

TEDDY. Wonderful moon. You could see everything. Not even our navigator could go wrong.

SWANSON. Any incidents ?

TEDDY. Turned intelligence officer on me, have you, Gloria ?

SWANSON. If you don't want to tell me——

TEDDY. No incidents, Gloria, if you exclude the fact that we had half our tail-plane shot away.

DUSTY. Wallowing about we were, coming home, like a fat old woman learning to swim. Fair turned me stomach.

TEDDY. Catted—did you, Dusty ?

DUSTY. Wasn't so bad for you, sir, up front.

TEDDY. It's never so bad for the driver, they say.

(MRS. OAKES *comes in with bacon and eggs and coffee on a tray.*)

MRS. OAKES (*coming down to the table. Politely*). Good morning, gentlemen.

TEDDY. 'Morning, Mrs. Oakes. What have you got there for us ? (*He lifts the cover off the dish. Joyfully.*) Eggs and bacon !

MRS. OAKES. I'd be glad if you wouldn't shout it to the entire hotel. I'm infringing regulations.

TEDDY. Mrs. Oakes, I could kiss you from head to foot.

MRS. OAKES. I trust you'll do nothing of the sort. (*She puts the coffee and one lot of eggs on the table.*)

TEDDY. Eggs, Dusty. Eggs ! You know what eggs are, don't you, or have you forgotten ?

DUSTY. You mean those round things that used to come out of hens in peace time ?

TEDDY (*sitting below fireplace*). That's right. Come and sit down, Pat. I could eat a house. I could eat you, Mrs. Oakes.

DORIS (*sharply*). Sh ! Quiet ! (*She rises and goes up to the window and listens intently.*) Sorry. Thought I heard a Wimpey.

MRS. OAKES. Is the Count not in yet ?

DORIS (*comes down to the sofa and picks up her shoes*). No, not yet. I think if you don't mind, duckies, I'll go up to my room. I can hear better from up there.

(*She goes up the stairs. An uncomfortable silence has fallen on the room.*)

(*From the landing.*) Save Johnny and me one of those eggs, won't you, dear ?

TEDDY. You bet.

(DORIS *goes out.*)

SWANSON. Any news of S Sugar ?

TEDDY. No. They're worried at ops. They were over the target twelve minutes before us—but they've heard nothing from them since.

(*A pause.*)

MRS. OAKES. I'll put this over here, by the fire.

(DUSTY *takes the tray and one dish and puts them on the fender.*)

If he comes in very late, knock on my door and I'll come down and make him some more. (*She goes up the stairs.*)

TEDDY. As usual, I can't thank you enough.

MRS. OAKES (*stops*). Don't be ridiculous. I dare say some people would be glad to have the chance of doing it. I'm going to bed, now. Good morning.

TEDDY. Good morning, Mrs. Oakes.

(MRS. OAKES *goes out.*)

SWANSON. Me for bed, too. Good show, Prune. Glad to see you back. Good night.

TEDDY. Good night, Gloria. (*Severely.*) I take an extremely poor view of your waiting up like this. Don't let it occur again.

SWANSON (*getting his hat and coat off the rack*). God, you don't think I waited up for you, do you ? Keeping the women company, that's all.

TEDDY. Then you're a dirty old man.

SWANSON (*to* PATRICIA). What did I tell you ? No respect. Shocking.

(*He goes out.*)

TEDDY. Come and sit down, boys and girls.

(PATRICIA *sits above the fire.* DUSTY *pushes her chair in.*)

Did you see the take-off ?

PATRICIA. Yes. (*She starts to arrange the coffee cups.*)

TEDDY. That crash was a bit of bad luck. It doesn't happen very often, you know. Plate, darling.

PATRICIA. I don't want anything to eat, thanks awfully.

TEDDY. On the level ?

PATRICIA. On the level. I couldn't, really.

TEDDY. All the more for us, eh Dusty ?

DUSTY. Well, sir, between you and me, I don't feel any too peckish myself. (*Rising, he goes up to the stairs.*)

TEDDY (*quickly*). Anything wrong ?

DUSTY. No, sir. Just that ride home. Cor, I still feel it down in the old darby kel. If you don't mind, sir, I think I'll go up and have a bit of shut-eye.

TEDDY. Poor old Dusty ! I'm awfully sorry. I *did* try and keep her steady, you know, but——

DUSTY (*strenuously*). Cor stuff me ! Going to say it's your fault now, I suppose ?

TEDDY. Well, it is, in a way.

DUSTY. Cor, stone me up an apple—— (*To* PATRICIA.) Isn't a skipper in the world would've brought us 'ome safe to-night, bar 'im, and he goes and apologizes for giving me stummick trouble. Cor, stuff me sideways, what a man !

TEDDY. Good night, Dusty.

DUSTY. Good night, sir.

(*He goes out.* TEDDY *is standing at the foot of the stairs.* PATRICIA *is still sitting at the table, her back to him, pouring out the coffee.*)

TEDDY (*murmuring*). Good old Dusty ! Don't you like old Dusty, darling ?

PATRICIA. Yes, Teddy. Very much.

TEDDY. Darling ?

PATRICIA. Yes, Teddy ?

TEDDY. I said, didn't you like old Dusty ?

PATRICIA. Yes, I said I did very much.

TEDDY. Did you ? (*He walks down to the sofa and bumps into the end of it ; then staggers and goes to the front of the sofa.*) Darling——

PATRICIA. Yes ?

TEDDY (*turns to face* PATRICIA). Where are you ?

(PATRICIA *turns her head sharply and looks at him for the first time.*)

PATRICIA (*rising*). Here, Teddy.

TEDDY. Where ? I can't see. Pat, come here. I want you.

PATRICIA. I'm here, Teddy. (*She catches him as he falls and kneels down beside him to support him. She looks round for help.*) Oh, God !

TEDDY. It's funny. I couldn't see you. I don't think I feel very well. It's nothing. Just a bit tired, that's all.

(*He fumbles at his breast pocket and pulls out a flask. He tries to open it but fails.* PATRICIA *takes it from him.*)

It twists sideways——

(PATRICIA *opens it. He tries to take the flask from her but she restrains him. She holds it while he drinks. He coughs and splutters.*)

Cherry brandy. Filthy stuff. Keeps you warm, though. (*He shakes his head.*) What are we doing kneeling down ? We look as if we were praying or something. (*He struggles to his feet and sinks on to the sofa.*) God, what an exhibition ! I'm sorry.

PATRICIA (*sits by him*). Do you feel well enough to go up to bed ?

TEDDY. I feel well enough, but I'm not going to. With eggs and bacon on the old menu—what an idea !

PATRICIA. You're ill. You're not just tired. You're ill. I'm going to ring up a doctor.

TEDDY. I'll murder you if you do. Come on. (*He crosses to the table and sits above it. His hands are still shaking.*) You watch me make a pig of myself. (*He picks up a knife and fork. Then he suddenly puts them down with a clatter and pushes the dish away.*) No good.

(PATRICIA *goes to the desk and looks in the directory.*)

What are you doing ? (*He rises.*)

PATRICIA. I'm going to get a doctor.

TEDDY (*crossing to her*). No, you don't. (*He grasps her hand.*)

PATRICIA. I'm sorry, Teddy. I must. (*She shakes her hand free and picks up the telephone.*)

TEDDY (*imploringly*). Don't, Pat, please . . .

PATRICIA. It's much better, Teddy. (*She lifts the receiver.*) Hullo . . . hullo . . .

TEDDY (*in a hard voice*). Do you want to get me chucked out of the Air Force.

PATRICIA. What do you mean ?

TEDDY. Put that receiver down.

(PATRICIA *replaces the receiver.*)

Come here.

(PATRICIA *walks slowly to him.*)

They always say a man should have no secrets from his wife, don't they ?

PATRICIA. Yes. Tell me.

TEDDY. All right. Do you know what's the matter with me ? Funk. Just ordinary, common or garden, plain bloody funk.

PATRICIA. Don't be absurd.

TEDDY. If a doctor examined me now, his diag—whatever it is—would be simply this. Here's a bloke who doesn't like flying.

PATRICIA (*stares at him, then smiles*). What about this ? (*She touches his D.F.C. ribbon.*)

TEDDY. The doc. would say to himself—bloke's got the D.F.C. Must have been all right once. Then he'd ask me— how many ops have you done, my lad ? Seventeen, sir. Doc. says to himself—bloke packs up after only seventeen trips, eh ? Just couldn't take it, I suppose. (*He goes down* L. *of the sofa.*)

PATRICIA (*follows him*). Don't talk nonsense, Teddy. The doctor would say—this man's ill. Probably nothing to do with flying at all. He ought to have a rest.

TEDDY (*bitterly*). A rest ? (*He sits on the sofa.*)

PATRICIA. What's wrong with that ?

TEDDY. There's nothing wrong with it. It's very nice—for some people. Ground job. Promotion probably. I'd have a fine time as a Squadron-Leader admin. at a training school— flaunting a D.F.C. and shooting a line with the pupils. The only thing is, some of the pupils might wonder why I'd only done seventeen trips before being grounded and a few of them might guess.

PATRICIA (*sitting on the* R. *arm of the sofa behind him*). In a case like this nobody would dare say a thing——

TEDDY. Only my friends. They'd say—Oh yes—Teddy Graham—not a bad bloke. Didn't like flying, that's all. And on my confidential report they'd put—grounded. Lack of moral fibre. That's the official phrase for—no guts.

PATRICIA (*angrily*). Listen, Teddy. There's no sense in all this. If you're too ill to fly——

TEDDY (*rising, crosses to the counter*). I'm not too ill to fly. I fly all right. You heard what Dusty said.

PATRICIA (*rising, crosses to him*). Yes, but it may not always be like that.

TEDDY. It will always be like that.

PATRICIA. What about your crew ? Is it fair on them ?

TEDDY (*turns to her, clenching his fists*). What's fair on my crew is my business.

PATRICIA. It's their lives you're risking as well as yours.

TEDDY. I'm their captain. Their captain. I wouldn't risk their lives.

PATRICIA. You are.

TEDDY (*crossing her to the* C. *table*). Don't, Pat, don't. You don't know—I can't bear it——

PATRICIA. I'm sorry, Teddy.

(*She puts her hand on his arm and sits by the table* R. *He turns down and falls at her feet. He lays his head on her lap and sobs.*)

Oh, my dear, my dear.

TEDDY (*his voice muffled by sobs*). A bloody Messerschmitt

put a cannon shell in our tail-plane—we went straight down in a dive—I heard Dusty on the intercomm.—He said—I thought I'd bought it, Skipper, but I'm all right—I'm all right ! We were in a vertical dive and I couldn't pull out—I couldn't pull out and Dusty said he was all right.

(*He is shaken by a further outburst of sobbing.* PATRICIA *strokes his head, saying nothing.*)

All the way back I had to fight to keep her on course—every one of them must have known it was odds against our getting home —but they trusted me—they trusted me—I heard the wireless op. say to the navigator—he's only just come on the crew—he said—don't worry, windy. Skipper'll get us home. Oh, my God ! Skipper'll get us home . . .

PATRICIA. You got them home.

TEDDY. You don't know what it's like to feel frightened. You get a beastly, bitter taste in the mouth, and your tongue goes dry and you feel sick, and all the time you're saying—This isn't happening—it can't be happening—I'll wake up. But you know you won't wake up. You know it is happening, and the sea's below you, and you're responsible for the lives of six people. And you have to pretend you're not afraid, that's what's so awful. Oh God, I was afraid to-night. When we took off and saw that kite on fire, I didn't think—There are friends of mine in that. I thought (*slowly*)—That might happen to us. Not very—pretty, is it ? (*He recovers himself slowly,* PATRICIA *watching him in silence. Then he turns away from her.*) Now you know it. Lack of moral fibre. I'm glad I told you. (*He rises.*)

PATRICIA. I'm glad, too.

TEDDY (*to* C.). Lend me a handkerchief.

(PATRICIA *gives him one from her pocket.* TEDDY *takes it, turns his back on her, and wipes his eyes. He sits on the sofa.*)

God, what you must think of me !

PATRICIA (*sits next to him*). Teddy, look at me.

(TEDDY *turns reluctantly to face her.*)

Why didn't you tell me all this before ?

TEDDY. I didn't want you to know you'd married a twirp.

PATRICIA. You damned little fool !

TEDDY. One exhibition's enough for to-night.

PATRICIA (*fiercely*). I'm all right.

TEDDY. Thank God I've had the courage to tell you. I couldn't tell anyone else in the world. I couldn't. But you help me, you see, so much——

PATRICIA (*angrily*). I don't help you at all. I've never tried to. How could I when you keep these things from me ?

TEDDY. You do help me—just by being—well—you—and incidentally by being my wife. It was you who got us home to-night. Not me.

PATRICIA (*desperately*). That's not true, Teddy. You're just saying that because you think I like to hear it. But it's not true.

TEDDY. Try leaving me and see what happens. (*A pause.*) I admit you've got every reason to, now. You must think you've got married under false pretences.

PATRICIA (*quietly*). No. I don't think that.

TEDDY. Thank you, Pat.

(*A pause.*)

PATRICIA (*gently*). I still think you should see a doctor. Someone who'll understand, and try and help you.

TEDDY. I don't need any help. Except yours. I do need that.

PATRICIA (*rises and goes up* R. *slightly*). Why go on with it, Teddy ? You've done your share. More than your share.

TEDDY (*slowly*). I have got quite a few more trips to do before I get given a rest.

PATRICIA. But there's no magic in any particular number. It may be more for some and less for others.

TEDDY. It may be more for me. It's not going to be less. We've got to win this war somehow, you know. God, how " Daily Mail " ! I'm glad nobody heard it but you. (*He gets up.*) You know, I feel better now than I've felt for months. I feel almost well enough to cope with Mrs. Oakes' bacon and eggs. (*He raises the cover and looks.*) No. I spoke too soon.

PATRICIA (*dully*). They must be cold by now. (*She sits on the* R. *arm of the sofa.*)

TEDDY. They are. I say—darling——

PATRICIA. Yes ?

TEDDY. Poor old Mrs. Oakes is going to be rather upset when she comes down in the morning and finds her precious eggs haven't been touched. I'd hate to hurt the old thing's feelings. (*He looks round.*) I know. (*He stares at the dish by the fire and then picks it up.*) I'd forgotten about old Johnny. If anything has happened to him, be kind to old Doris, won't you ? I'm not much good at saying the right things on these occasions. We'd better leave it there, just in case. (*He puts the dish down again and takes the shovel from the fire.*) I won't be long. I'm just going to have a look at the garden.

(*He goes out of the front door with the shovel and the covered dish from the breakfast table.* PATRICIA *sits, without moving.* PETER *comes down the stairs in a dressing-gown.*)

PETER (*down behind the sofa*). I heard his voice. He got back all right, then ?

PATRICIA. Yes.

PETER. I'm glad. Poor Pat! You must have had a rough night.

(*He takes her hand. She withdraws it, sharply ; he stares at her, surprised. She stands up and then crosses to the foot of the stairs. There is a pause. Then* TEDDY *comes in, with the dish in his hands.*)

TEDDY. Hullo!

PETER (*coming up to him*). Hullo! I'm glad to see you back.

TEDDY. Thanks.

PETER (*indicating the dish*). What are you doing with that ?

TEDDY. I've been burying six fried eggs, and twelve rashers of bacon, in a flower bed. Crazy type, you see, old Graham. By the way, it's broad daylight. Look.

(*Lighting Cue No.* 3 : *Lights in room fade.*)

(*He pulls back the window curtains, admitting the morning sun. Then he lays the dish on the table and puts the shovel in the fireplace, and goes up to* PATRICIA.) Come on, darling. Time we were in bed.

(*He takes her hand and leads her up the stairs.* PETER *watches them from below.*)

CURTAIN.

ACT III

SCENE.—*The same, about* 12 *noon, the same morning.*

DORIS *is sitting in the armchair above the fire, reading a magazine.*
PERCY *enters from the bar, carrying a tray with five clean ashtrays
on it. He puts the tray on the counter, crosses to the* C. *table,
picks up the coffee tray and puts it on the counter.*

PERCY. Twelve o'clock, Countess. Bar's open.

DORIS (*abstractedly*). What ? Oh, thank you, Percy.

(*During the next speech* PERCY *puts the clean ashtrays on the
tables* R., C. *and up* L., *in that order.*)

PERCY. Fun and games last night, eh ? That Wiggy Jones !
He's a one, eh ? That song—"I don't want to join the Air
Force " ! That's a song, eh ? Been trying to remember it all
the morning.

DORIS. You'd better forget it, Percy. It's not a song for
little boys.

PERCY. Garn with your little boys ! Bit of a do up at the
aerodrome last night, eh ? Did you 'ear 'bout it ? One got
shot down taking off. (*He moves down* L. *with an ashtray for the
fender.*)

DORIS. I saw it.

PERCY. Did you ? Coo, wish I 'ad. (*He takes the ashtray
to the radio table.*) I saw the wreckage this morning, though.
Burnt right out, it was. 'Orrible. (*In a confidential whisper.*)
Where was it last night, do you know ? (*He crosses to the counter
for the coffee tray.*)

DORIS. Eight o'clock news said it was the Rhineland.

PERCY (*dusting the counter*). Rhineland, eh ? It was Rhineland last time they went. I knew something was up when they
didn't come down to dinner. Flight-Lieutenant Graham, 'e
tried to fox me. Nothing on to-night, Percy, 'e said. 'Ome
sweet 'ome to-night. I knew 'e was keeping something up 'is
sleeve. Count went too, didn't 'e ?

DORIS. Yes. He went.

PERCY. 'Ow is 'e this morning ? All right ?

DORIS. He hasn't come back yet.

(*There is a pause.* PERCY *stares at her unbelievingly.*)

PERCY. Not come back ?

DORIS. Of course they may have force-landed somewhere.

PERCY (*crossing to her*). That's what's 'appened, you mark
my words. Count's not one to get 'imself shot down by those
dirty 'uns.

59

DORIS. I'm afraid, though, Percy, if they had force-landed, they'd have let Milchester know.

(*There is another pause.*)

PERCY. Coo, I'm sorry, Countess.

DORIS. That's all right, Percy.

PERCY. I seen 'em go off night after night, and they always got back. Never thought they wouldn't, some'ow. 'Course you'd 'ear it on the wireless—" Some of our aircraft failed to return." Never thought it'd 'appen to us, though. Coo! Makes yer think, don't it ? (*He stands uncertainly.*) Anything I can get you, Countess ? Gin and lime or anything ?

DORIS. No, thanks.

PERCY. I'll see it's on the 'ouse.

DORIS. No, Percy. Ta, all the same.

(PERCY *goes into the lounge.* MRS. OAKES *comes in from the coffee-room.*)

MRS. OAKES. Any news, Countess ? (*Moving to the* L. *end of the sofa.*)

DORIS. No, not yet. The Squadron-Leader is going to let me know as soon as he hears anything.

MRS. OAKES. I expect he'll come back all right. Do you feel it cold in here, Countess ? Would you like a fire ?

DORIS. No, thanks. It's a lovely day, really. Like summer.

(PETER *comes in through the front door.*)

MRS. OAKES (*to* PETER, *moving above the sofa*). I saw you admiring our garden, Mr. Kyle. How do you like it ?

PETER (*perfunctorily*). Very much. Is Mrs. Graham still not down ?

MRS. OAKES. I don't think so. I haven't seen her.

PETER. But it's nearly lunchtime.

MRS. OAKES (*crossing to the counter*). Just gone twelve.

PETER (*coming down to* L. *of* MRS. OAKES). I suppose you couldn't—— (*He stops.*)

MRS. OAKES. Couldn't what, Mr. Kyle ?

PETER. It doesn't matter. I'll wait.

(MRS. OAKES *opens the flap of the counter.*)

(*Brusquely.*) Get me a whisky-and-soda, please. (*He sits by the table* R.)

MRS. OAKES (*turns to him*). That's hardly my province. (*She goes to* the *door of the bar. Calling.*) Percy !

PERCY (*appearing at the lounge door*). Yes, mum ?

MRS. OAKES. A whisky-and-soda for Mr. Kyle.

PERCY. Yes, mum. There's no whisky, mum.

MRS. OAKES (*to* PETER). There's no whisky.

PETER. Is there any brandy ?

MRS. OAKES (*to* PERCY). Is there any brandy ?

PERCY. Yes, mum.

PETER. Brandy-and-soda, then.

MRS. OAKES. Brandy-and-soda, Percy.

PERCY. Yes, mum.

(PERCY'S *head disappears.* MRS. OAKES *walks to the door of her office.*)

MRS. OAKES. The next time you're requiring a drink, will you be good enough to press the bell marked " Waiter " ?

(PETER *does not answer.* MRS. OAKES *goes out.* PETER *is engaged in reading some pencilled sheets of paper, which look as if they had been torn from a pocket book.* PERCY *comes in with a brandy-and-soda.*)

PERCY (*puts it on the table* R.). Brandy-and-soda, sir. Three and six.

PETER (*looking up*). What ? Oh, all right. (*He throws two coins on to the tray with a clatter.*) Keep the change.

PERCY. Thank you, sir. Thank you. (*He pockets the change and brings out something else. He goes up to* DORIS *and shows it to her.*) Countess.

(DORIS *rises and looks in his hand.*)

DORIS. What's this, Percy ?

PERCY. Bele. An Indian god. Bought 'im at a fair. You hold 'im in your right 'and, and whatever you wish comes true.

DORIS. Oh. (*She puts it in her right hand, holds it a second and returns it to him.*) Thanks, Percy.

PERCY. No. You keep 'im. It don't work if it's not yours.

DORIS. Don't you want him ?

PERCY. No. You keep him. (*He crosses to* C. *and then turns back to her.*) Just been thinking. Count might 'ave baled out over the other side, then 'e'd be a prisoner of war.

DORIS. No, he's a Pole. I'd rather anything than that.

PERCY. I suppose you're right.

(DORIS *crosses to the fire.* PERCY *goes out.* PETER *stuffs the sheets of paper into his pocket and stands up. He looks at* DORIS. *He clears his throat.*)

PETER (*rises*). I heard about your husband from Mrs. Oakes. I'm most terribly sorry——

DORIS (*crossing to him* L.C.). Thank you, Mr. Kyle, but I've not given up yet. What I always say is, while there's life there's —hope.

(SWANSON *has come in quickly and* DORIS *speaks the last word looking straight at him over* PETER'S *shoulder. Her voice falters.* PETER *turns round.*)

SWANSON. 'Morning, Kyle. Do you mind if I see the Countess alone for a moment ?

PETER. No. Not at all. (*He takes his drink off the table* R. *and goes to the lounge door.*) If Mrs. Graham comes down will you tell her that I want to see her—most urgently. It's very important.

SWANSON. Right. I'll tell her.

(PETER *goes into the lounge.* SWANSON, *as he comes down* R.C., *does not look at* DORIS, *who has not taken her eyes off his face.*)

DORIS (*at length*). Come on, dear. Let's have it.

SWANSON. Well, I'm afraid it may be rather a shock——

DORIS. That's all right. I've had the shock. Tell us.

SWANSON. Your husband's aircraft did send out a signal this morning, at approximately four-twenty-five. It said simply : Am force-landing on the sea. Then they sent out call signs for about ten minutes, and the D.F. stations got a pretty accurate fix on them. Then nothing more was heard. Since daylight this morning aircraft and power boats—the Air Sea Rescue chaps—have been out looking for them, and about half an hour ago they signalled us that the wreckage of a Wellington bomber had been found—within three miles of the spot fixed by the D.F. people. So I'm afraid it looks—— (*He stops.*) They're continuing the search : they had a rubber dinghy on board and it's just possible they might have been picked up by some vessel which hadn't a wireless or any way of letting us know.

(DORIS *shakes her head.*)

DORIS. It's better not to think of loopholes. I'm quite ready to face it. Johnny's dead.

SWANSON (*automatically*). You're very brave.

DORIS. That's the second time that's been said to me since last night. It isn't true. I'm just—ready, that's all. (*She goes to the armchair for her bag.*)

(PATRICIA *comes down the stairs.* DORIS *moves again towards* SWANSON.)

Thanks for taking all this trouble, Squadron-Leader. I know what a bind it must be, breaking bad news to people. (*She goes up the stairs and comes face to face with* PATRICIA.) Hullo, ducks.

PATRICIA. I overheard what you said. Is it—Johnny ?

DORIS (*as she goes up the stairs*). Yes, dear. They found bits of poor old S Sugar floating in the drink. It looks as if he's bought it all right.

(*She goes out.*)

PATRICIA. Is there no hope ?

SWANSON. Officially, yes. Unofficially——— (*He shakes his head.*) She prefers to take the unofficial view, and I dare say it's better she should. (*A pause.*) Well, I must be going. (*He goes up to the door.*) Sunday papers haven't come ; and I've volunteered to go down to the village to collect them.

PATRICIA (*coming down behind the sofa*). Is there a chemist in the village that's open on Sunday ?

SWANSON. We can beat one up for you, if you like—why ?

PATRICIA. I want to get some stuff for Teddy's wrist. Are you driving in ? Will you give me a lift ?

SWANSON. Yes, but do you mind waiting five minutes ? I've got to dash up to the station first.

PATRICIA. That's all right. (*She leaves her bag on the sofa, and crosses to the fire.*) Whenever you're going.

SWANSON. I'll get cracking. (*At the door.*) How is he this morning ?

PATRICIA (*sits on the fender*). A bit tired, I think. They had rather a shaky do last night.

SWANSON. Shaky do ? Learning the old vernacular, eh ? Well, I'll dash. Oh, by the way, Kyle's waiting for you in there. (*He points to the bar.*) Says it's most important.

PATRICIA. Oh, thank you.

SWANSON. Won't keep you long.

(SWANSON *goes out.* PATRICIA *looks, undecided, at the bar door. Then she turns quickly to go back upstairs. The bar door opens and* PETER *comes out.* PATRICIA, *half-way up the stairs, turns slowly.*)

PATRICIA. Peter—please—I don't want to see you. I told you———

PETER (*crossing to the banisters*). You're going to see me.

PATRICIA. Not now. I'll come up to London, I'll see you there. I'll explain———

PETER. Explain what ? Five little bits of paper dumped on my bed with my morning tea, and you expected me to jump on the first train up to London and fade quietly out of your life muttering " it's a far, far better thing "—(*bitterly*)—who's living in a film world, you or me ?

PATRICIA. I was coming to see you in London. I had to write it down because it helped me to think. I couldn't have said it. I can't say it now. I'm sorry I wrote it though, Pete, it wasn't awfully brave.

PETER. - You really want me to take this letter seriously ?

PATRICIA. Yes, Pete.

PETER. This is how seriously I take it. (*He tears the letter up into small pieces.*) Never play this sort of trick on me again as long as you live. If you have any more of these bouts of

conscience or—whatever it is (*crossing down* R.) come and tell
me—but for the love of God don't send me any more notes by
any more chambermaids. I've had the worst morning of my
life. (*He turns his back on her.*)

PATRICIA. Try and understand, Pete, I'm not doing this for
fun.

(PETER *turns.*)

PETER. Doing what ?

PATRICIA. Leaving you.

(*There is a pause.* PETER *stares at her unbelievingly.*)

PETER. Shut up, Pat, don't talk nonsense.

PATRICIA. I'm leaving you, Pete.

(PETER *puts his cigarette out and takes a step towards her.*)

PETER. Why ?

PATRICIA. I've told you. Teddy needs me.

PETER. Do you think I don't ?

PATRICIA. He's my husband. (*Coming down to the fire.*)

PETER (*bitterly*). That's very good. (*Crossing to her.*) In
your letter you say that it's your duty to stay with your husband.
You did say duty, didn't you ?

PATRICIA (*facing the fire*). I don't know, I can't remember.

PETER. You did say duty. Your duty to him, or to me, or
to yourself, or to your country, or to what—what does duty
mean, anyway ? I'm sorry, Pat, I don't understand, really I
don't.

PATRICIA. I didn't think you would, Pete.

PETER. I know you don't feel anything for him, you've told
me so.

PATRICIA. Did I ?

PETER (*he looks at her startled*). What was it you found out
last night ?

PATRICIA. I can't tell you. It wasn't only about Teddy, it
was something about myself too, something I didn't know before.
(*Desperately. Crossing to him* C.). I can't explain myself, Pete,
I told you I wouldn't be able to.

PETER (*stopping her* C., *urgently*). You've got to try.

PATRICIA. I can't—I can't (*turning to go*).

(PETER *turns her round to face him.*)

PETER. You must explain yourself. You're leaving me.
Why ? (PATRICIA *says nothing.*) You're leaving me. Do you
understand what that's going to mean to me ? This isn't some
ordinary little intrigue, that can be smashed in a second, this is
something that's vitally important.

PATRICIA. No !

PETER. What ?

PATRICIA. This isn't important. We thought it was, but it isn't, not now anyway. That's one of the things I found out last night. (*She stops uncertainly.*)

PETER (*quietly*). Go on.

PATRICIA (*crossing to the chair by the table* R.). I was awfully sure about things until last night. I had made a fool of myself once before, that time I ran away from you, because of conventions and what other people said and thought. I made up my mind, never again. (*She turns to face* PETER.) You know that. I used to think that our private happiness was something far too important to be affected by outside things, like the war or marriage vows.

PETER. Yes it is, Pat, far too important.

PATRICIA. No, it isn't, Pete, beside what's happening out there (*she points to the window*) its just tiny and rather—cheap— I'm afraid. (*She crosses back to* R. *of* PETER.) I don't want to believe that. I'm an awful coward. It may be just my bad luck, but I've suddenly found that I'm in that battle and I can't——

PETER. Desert ?

PATRICIA. Yes, desert.

PETER. Very heroic.

PATRICIA. I'm sorry if it sounded like that, heaven knows it's far from the truth.

PETER (*after a pause*). Pat, listen to me, you say you love me. I know that's true. I love you too, but more than that I need you so much that if you go away from me now, I just don't know what I'm going to do. That's not a line, Pat, the sort of thing one says at a moment like *this*, it's true—I just don't know what I'm going to do.

PATRICIA. Oh, Pete—— (*She takes his shoulders.*)

PETER. Come with me, Pat, we'll go away, we'll forget about Teddy——

PATRICIA (*moves up slightly*). No !

(*There is a long pause.*)

PETER (*turns away from her. At length*). Haven't you forgotten something ?

PATRICIA. What ?

PETER. I'm desperate, Pat. I'll do anything in the world to stop you leaving me.

PATRICIA (*stating a fact*). No, Pete, you wouldn't do that.

PETER. Where is Teddy ?

PATRICIA. Upstairs.

PETER. Will you go up now and tell him that you're coming away with me ?

PATRICIA. No.

PETER (*calling*). Percy !

(PERCY *appears.* PATRICIA *sits on the table* c.)

PERCY. Sir ?
PETER. Go and tell Flight-Lieutenant Graham that I'd like to see him.
PERCY. Yes, sir. (*He goes to the top of the stairs.*)
PETER. Tell him that it's important.
PERCY. Yes, sir, I'll tell him.

(*He goes out.*)

PATRICIA (*quietly*). I could deny it, you know.
PETER. It won't be difficult to prove.
PATRICIA. Whatever you tell him won't force me to leave Teddy.
PETER. Won't it ? I think that's for Teddy to say.

(*There is a pause.*)

PATRICIA. You won't do it, Pete.

(SWANSON *comes in through the front door.*)

SWANSON (*in the doorway*). All ready, Mrs. Graham ? Haven't been long, have I ?

(PATRICIA *is staring at* PETER.)

PATRICIA (*rising*). What ? No, you've been very quick.

(PERCY *runs down the stairs.*)

PERCY. Flight-Lieutenant Graham's in his bath, sir. Says he'll be down directly.
PETER. Right. Thank you.

(PERCY *goes out.*)

SWANSON. Well, we'd better get leaving, or we'll find this chemist feller has gone to lunch.
PETER. I don't think Mrs. Graham's going with you, after all. Are you, Mrs. Graham ? Didn't you say you had to stay in ?

(*A pause.* PATRICIA *goes behind the sofa and picks up her bag and moves up to the door.*)

PATRICIA. No, I'm not staying in. I must get that stuff for Teddy.

(SWANSON, *a little puzzled, holds the door open for her.*)

SWANSON. I can get it for you, quite easily, you know—if you'd rather stay behind.
PATRICIA. Thank you, but I'd rather come with you.

(PETER *is staring at her. She goes out quickly.* SWANSON *follows
her. Exit* PATRICIA *and* SWANSON. PETER, *left alone, goes to
the window and lights a cigarette.* DUSTY's *and* MAUDIE's
voices can be heard outside. PETER *goes to the window seat.*
DUSTY *and* MAUDIE *come in.* DORIS *comes down the stairs and
sits below the fire, reading a letter.*)

DUSTY (*hanging up his hat*). Aunt Ella's all right if you treat
'er all right. There's nothing wrong with Aunt Ella.
MAUDIE (*down* R.). You don't have to live with her, Dave.
DUSTY. You need tact, Maudie, that's all, just a bit of tact.
MAUDIE (*firmly*). You need a frying pan—that's what you
need. (*She crosses to the stairs.*)
DUSTY. That's the wrong attitude. What I say is——   (*He
catches sight of* PETER.) Oh, good morning, sir.
PETER (*shortly*). Good morning.
DUSTY. Nice day, isn't it ?

(MAUDIE *has walked across towards the stairs, which she is now
mounting.* DUSTY *crosses to the foot of the stairs.*)

Where you going, Maudie ?
MAUDIE. Up to our room. I've got my packing to do.
DUSTY. Heavens, Maudie, you don't want to pack yet.
You've got loads of time. 'Bus doesn't go till one.
MAUDIE. I don't want to miss it, Dave.

(DUSTY *chases her up the stairs.*)

DUSTY. You won't miss it, Maudie, that I promise.
MAUDIE. If I don't get packed, I will miss it.
DUSTY. But you 'aven't got nothing to pack, bar one nighty
and a toothbrush——

(MAUDIE *disappears.*)

(*To* PETER.) Women !

(*He goes out.* PETER *sees* DORIS *and walks across to the bar door,* R.)

DORIS (*rising*). Mr. Kyle ? (*She moves to* C.)

(PETER *turns.*)

PETER. Yes ?
DORIS. Are you good at languages ?
PETER. I know French and Spanish and some German.
Why ?
DORIS. Can you tell me what language this is written in ?

(PETER *goes to her* C.)

(*She hands him a letter.*) It isn't Polish, that's all I know.
PETER (*glancing at the letter*). It's French. '*He hands the
letter back.*)

DORIS. Yes, of course. He spoke French like he spoke Polish. I suppose he thought it'd be easier for me to get translated.

PETER. It's from your husband ?

DORIS. He left it with me. I was only to read it if something happened to him. Funny—it's the only letter I've ever had from him.

(PETER *goes to the bar door again.* DORIS *looks at the letter, knitting her brows.*)

Oh, Mr. Kyle, you know French. Will you read it for me ?

PETER. Do you mind ? I'd rather not.

(DORIS *stands uncertainly looking up the stairs.* PETER *changes his mind and takes the letter from her.*)

DORIS. Thanks, Mr. Kyle, dear. Sorry if it's a bother. (*She crosses him to the chair by the table* R.) If there's anything in it that's—well—you know—you won't tell anyone, will you ?

PETER. No.

DORIS (*sits*). Of course you wouldn't. Okay, dear. Go ahead.

PETER. It begins—" It will be necessary for you——"

DORIS. Doesn't he start with dear Doris, or anything ?

PETER. No.

DORIS. The French for dear is chère, isn't it ? That's the only French word I do know. All right, go on.

PETER (*translating slowly*). " It will be necessary for you to translate "—no—" to have this letter translated. I do not yet express myself in your language well enough to say what I wish to say to you. I am not able to leave you without telling you what your kindness and devotion have meant to me——"

DORIS. Silly.

PETER. " Since the murder of my wife and boy in Varsovie——"

DORIS. That's Warsaw. The Nazis machine-gunned them, just as they were leaving——

PETER. " —I did not think to feel——" It's rather difficult this. (*He sits on the sofa.*) I think he means : " I did not think I would feel any human emotion again——" That's not quite right, I'm afraid.

DORIS. I know what he means. Go on.

PETER. " I came to your country with only one thought, to continue to fight against the Germans until I myself found the death in battle which I——"

DORIS. Yes ?

PETER. " —have—sought—for a long time. It was not always easy, living in a strange country—and would at first have seemed intolerable—if I had not had the—blessed—good fortune to meet you, my beloved wife——''

DORIS. Chère ?

PETER. No. Bien-aimée. Well-loved.

DORIS. I see. Go on.

PETER. '' I found in you what I had lost in Warsaw—I had thought for ever—an—understanding and a sympathy ''—sympathie means something a little different to sympathy. It's rather hard to translate.

DORIS. I think I know what it means.

PETER. '' —an understanding and a sympathy so strong ''—powerful—'' that the words we neither of us could speak did not need to be spoken. I can only thank you with a full heart—and it is with real sorrow that I take my leave of you now. I would have so much wished to have repaid you for the sacrifice you made for my sake, in giving up your career—as hotel-keeper——''

DORIS. Hotel-keeper ?

PETER. Hotelière.

DORIS. I was a barmaid, dear. I was behind the bar when I first met him. The Crown at Pulborough. He came into the Public Bar one night and said he was lost, only nobody could understand him. I walked with him as far as where he was going. When he said good night he kissed my hand. He came into the Crown a lot after that—always the Public, I don't know why. Hotel-keeper. That's Johnny all over. Sorry, dear. Go on.

PETER. '' I would have so much wished to have repaid you for your sacrifice—by taking you with me, after the war, to Poland, where I might, in some very small measure, have been able to make a return to you of the material debt I owe you : the other debt I can never repay. Good-bye, my dear, dear wife. I love you for ever.'' (PETER *finishes translating, folds the letter up, puts it back into the envelope and puts it on* DORIS'S *lap.*)

DORIS. Ta. (*She puts the letter in her bag and gets up.* PETER *is purposely not looking at her. She crosses to* C., *then turns to* PETER.) I shan't forget the way you did that. You made it sound very nice. (*She reaches the stairs and stops.*) Oh, Mr. Kyle, that last bit. You didn't make it up, did you ?

PETER. No. It's in the letter. You can get anyone to translate it for you.

DORIS. Thanks, dear. Just so long as I know.

(*She goes out upstairs.* MRS. OAKES *enters from the coffee-room, some sheets over her arm. She bends down at the foot of the stairs and picks up the scraps of paper which* PETER *had torn up in his scene with* PATRICIA.)

MRS. OAKES (*clicking her teeth disapprovingly*). What's this ? A paper-chase ?

PETER. They're mine. (*He takes the scraps of paper from her and stuffs them in his pocket.*)

MRS. OAKES. Waste-paper receptacles are provided, Mr. Kyle. Besides, there's such a thing as salvage, you know.

PETER. I'm sorry. It was very untidy of me. (*He moves up to the window.*)

(MRS. OAKES *goes up the stairs, meeting* TEDDY, *who comes running down, dressed in ordinary uniform, not battledress.*)

TEDDY. Hullo, you old dusky enchantress. We made rather a hole in your bacon and eggs last night, eh ?

(MRS. OAKES *glances round hurriedly at* PETER.)

MRS. OAKES. By which you mean the sausages, I suppose.

TEDDY. That's right. The sausages. Delicious.

MRS. OAKES. I'm glad you liked them, I'm sure.

(*She goes up the stairs and out.*)

TEDDY (*crosses to the bar. To* PETER). You wanted to see me about something, didn't you ?

PETER. Yes, I did.

TEDDY. Any objection if I order a beer first ? I've got a thirst on.

PETER. Go ahead. (*He moves down* L.C.)

TEDDY. Anything for you ?

PETER (*down* L.). No, thank you.

(TEDDY *goes to the bar door.*)

TEDDY. A somewhat boozy type, old Graham, I'm afraid. (*Calling.*) Hey, Percy. Bring me a beer, and jump to it !

PERCY (*off*). Yes, Mr. Graham, sir.

TEDDY (*to* PETER, *moving up* R.). Bad show about Johnny, isn't it ?

PETER. Yes. I'm very sorry. (*Crossing to above the sofa.*)

TEDDY. He was good value, old Johnny. One of the very best. (*A pause.*) They're a bit different from us, these Poles, you know. Crazy types, most of them. They're only really happy when they're having a crack at Jerry.

PETER. The same doesn't apply to you ?

TEDDY. Not exactly. I'm quite ready to admit we some-times find it a bit of a bind.

(PERCY *comes in with a half-pint of beer.*)

Well, bung ho ! (*He takes a gulp of beer.*) Chalk it up, Percy.

PERCY. Yes, sir. (*He goes out.*)

TEDDY. Okay, Kyle. Shoot. Give us the five-second burst. (PETER *does not reply.*) Go ahead. What have you got to say to me ?

PETER. Nothing.

TEDDY. What do you mean, nothing ?

PETER. Nothing. Just good-bye. I'm leaving this morning.

TEDDY. Oh, sorry to hear it. Percy told me it was some-thing important.

PETER. He must have got it wrong. It's quite unimportant.

TEDDY (*crossing to him, contrite*). I say, I'm most frightfully sorry. I didn't mean that, you know. I mean, you'll be coming down again, won't you ?

PETER. No. I'm leaving on the Clipper within a few days. You won't see me again.

TEDDY (*sitting on the* R. *arm of the sofa*). Wish I was a film star.

PETER. Do you ?

TEDDY. Dashing madly about all over the world, pursued by fans, making pots of money, glamorous females hurling themselves at you wherever you go.

PETER (*crossing to the fire, crumpling up the fine pieces of paper*). It's not so much fun as it sounds.

TEDDY. Not exactly a bind, though. I say, I nearly forgot. (*He rises, fumbles in his pockets and produces a notebook.*) You've got to write something in my book.

PETER. I'd rather not, if you don't mind.

TEDDY. What do you mean, you'd rather not ? I'll take it as a personal affront.

PETER. It's only that I don't know what to say.

TEDDY. Say anything—preferably something I can shoot a line about. You know—to my life-long buddy—or—to the whitest man I ever knew. (*Crossing to* PETER.) No, what about—to Teddy Graham, dauntless eagle of the skies, from his humble admirer and friend——

PETER (*suddenly losing control*). For God's sake, shut up !

(TEDDY *starts. There is a pause.*)

TEDDY. Sorry. Only my warped sense of humour, you know.

(PETER *snatches the book, scribbles something in it hurriedly and returns it to* TEDDY.)

Thanks a lot. (*He reads it.*) Oh, thanks. Between you and me I never know what that means, although it's the Air Force motto.

PETER. I don't know what it means, either.

(*He crosses to the* R. *table as* TEDDY *puts the notebook away.*)

Sorry for the outburst. I don't feel too well this morning.

TEDDY (*sympathetically*). You don't look any too well. Hardly the smooth, glamorous lover of the screen. Sorry. Is that a brick ?

PETER. Yes. I'm getting old, you see, Teddy, and that's something I don't care to be reminded of.

(PATRICIA *comes in. She stands just inside the door.*)

TEDDY. Hullo, darling. Did you get that stuff ?

PATRICIA. Yes. (*She moves down to the* C. *table.*) It wasn't what you asked for, but the chemist said it was just as good. (*She hands him a packet.*)

TEDDY. Thanks most awfully. Kyle's leaving us this morning. Did you know ? (*He undoes the parcel.*)

(PATRICIA *looks at* PETER.)

PATRICIA. Yes. He told me.

TEDDY. He's off on the Clipper in a couple of days. Lucky type, isn't he ?

PATRICIA. Yes. (*She sits on the* R. *end of the sofa.*)

(TEDDY *occupies himself with the parcel. There is a pause.* PETER *turns abruptly and makes for the stairs.* MRS. OAKES *comes down simultaneously.*)

PETER (*to* MRS. OAKES). Oh, Mrs. Oakes, can you get me a car, please ?

MRS. OAKES. Yes, Mr. Kyle. When do you want it ?

PETER. As soon as possible.

MRS. OAKES. I'll do my best.

(PETER *goes out.*)

(*Crossing to* R.). He looks ill—Mr. Kyle. Is anything the matter with him ?

TEDDY. It's that dinner you gave him last night, I expect.

MRS. OAKES. Indeed it isn't. I had the rissoles myself, and there's nothing wrong with me.

TEDDY (*follows her*). We haven't all got your cast-iron stomach.

(MRS. OAKES *slams down the flap of the counter and goes out into her office.* TEDDY *crosses behind the sofa and kisses* PATRICIA *on the cheek.*)

You don't look any too well, yourself, this morning. Do you feel all right ?

PATRICIA. Oh, I'm all right. When will you be flying again ?

TEDDY. Don't know. Not for two or three days, anyway. They'll be working on that tail-plane of ours. Next time I go on a trip, I suppose you'll be back in London.

PATRICIA. No. I won't.

TEDDY. Don't give me heart failure. You mean you're going to stay down here ?

PATRICIA. Yes, Teddy, if you want me to.

TEDDY. Don't be an utter clot, darling ! If I want you to !
God, how marvellous ! How long will you stay ?

PATRICIA. For good.

TEDDY. For good—but what about your new play ? Aren't
you starting rehearsals next week ?

PATRICIA. No, I'm not going to do it, I'm turning it down.

TEDDY. You'll give up the flat ?

PATRICIA. Yes.

TEDDY. Oh boy ! Yippee !

(*He vaults into the sofa.* PATRICIA *watches him, unsmiling.*
    TEDDY *pulls himself up short, a trifle crestfallen.*)

I say, Pat,—you're not doing this because of—because of——

PATRICIA. No, Teddy. I want to stay with you. (*She
approaches* TEDDY *with a bandage and a bottle of iodine.*) I
think I'd better do this now.

TEDDY. All right, Nurse. (*He bares his wrist.*) I warn you
I shall scream.

(PATRICIA *dabs iodine on his wrist.*)

PATRICIA. Sorry.

TEDDY. It doesn't hurt at all. (*Suddenly.*) Ow ! D.A.

PATRICIA. D.A. ?

TEDDY. Delayed action.

(PATRICIA *begins to bandage the wrist.*)

PATRICIA. I'm not very good at this, I'm afraid.

TEDDY. You're much too beautiful to be good at bandaging.

PATRICIA. Teddy ?

TEDDY. Yes, darling ?

PATRICIA. You have been rather an awful fool, you know.

TEDDY. Have I ?

PATRICIA. We've been married nearly a year now.

TEDDY. You're telling me.

PATRICIA. We don't know each other awfully well, do we ?

TEDDY. No, I suppose we don't—at least I know you all
right—every little bit of you—but I admit I have been a bit of
a dark horse with you. But now, after last night——

PATRICIA. Last night isn't enough. It's not enough unless
you go on telling me things—unless you——

TEDDY. What ?

PATRICIA. Unless you treat me more like a wife and less like
a show-piece.

TEDDY (*shocked*). Show-piece ?

PATRICIA (*slowly*). Suggested that Flight-Lieutenant Graham
shall in future be permitted to mention his wife's name not more
than—how many times—per diem—ten—was it ?

TEDDY. Oh, Gawd ! How did you hear about that ?

PATRICIA. It doesn't matter.

TEDDY. I'll kill Gloria.

PATRICIA. He thought—I'd be pleased. I was too—in a way —but—well, you see what I mean, don't you ?

TEDDY. God ! Tear me off a strip, I deserve it.

PATRICIA. No, you don't. It's not really been your fault, at least it's been much more mine than yours.

TEDDY. Oh, darling, what utter bilge ! It's not been your fault at all.

PATRICIA. It doesn't much matter whose fault it's been, Teddy, does it, providing we both make a bit of an effort from now on. There—— (*She finishes bandaging.*)

TEDDY. Thanks, awfully. Darling, talking about show-piece—— Well, when I first asked you to marry me, I never thought you'd say yes, and when you did, I could never quite believe there hadn't been a mistake somewhere. And so I've always been a bit scared of you. And when we've been together, I've always been afraid of boring you—and so I tried awfully hard not to bore and so, of course, I always did bore you—and that is why show-piece is just about right, I suppose. But now, after last night, well——

PATRICIA. Go on, Teddy.

TEDDY. Well, it's just that I do love—and I don't know— somehow, I'm not scared of you any more.

(DUSTY *and* MAUDIE *come down the stairs,* DUSTY *carrying* MAUDIE'S *suitcase.*)

DUSTY. 'Morning, sir.

TEDDY (*rises*). 'Morning, Sergeant. How's the old tum ?

DUSTY (*down between* MAUDIE *and* TEDDY). Not so bad, sir. Feels 'ellish empty, though.

(PATRICIA *wraps up the parcel.*)

TEDDY. Needs refuelling, I expect. Hullo, Mrs. Miller. How are you this morning ?

MAUDIE. Very well, thank you, Mr. Graham. Dave and I went for a walk and he showed me your Wellington.

TEDDY (*startled*). What ? How did you get her past the guards ?

DUSTY. She only saw it from the road, sir. It's still out at dispersal.

MAUDIE (*accusingly*). Did you know that it's got a big hole in its tail ?

DUSTY (*hastily*). 'Course he knew, Maudie. He's only the jolly old skipper.

MAUDIE (*firmly*). Yes, but you told me that he sits up there in front. He might not have known what was going on at the back.

TEDDY.   I don't usually, Mrs. Miller, but as a matter of fact
I did know about the hole.

MAUDIE.   I thought you ought to know, Mr. Graham ; that's
why I told you.   It looks very dangerous—a great big hole like
that.

TEDDY.   Thank you, Mrs. Miller.   You were quite right to
tell me.   We're going to have it seen to.

MAUDIE.   I'm very glad to hear it.

(*Enter the* COUNT *at the door up* R.)

DUSTY.   You must forgive my wife, sir.   I'm afraid she don't
know much about aircraft.

TEDDY.   That's all right, Dusty.   My wife doesn't either.

MAUDIE.   I do know about aircraft—I know which are ours—
which are theirs.

TEDDY.   I wish Dusty—Dave were as hot on aircraft recogni-
tion.

(*During the last few lines the* COUNT *has been standing just inside
the door, taking off his flying jacket.   He is in full flying kit,
dishevelled, dirty and damp.   He waits patiently for a lull in the
conversation before launching himself into speech.*)

COUNT (R.C.).   Is—please—my wife—in home ?

TEDDY.   Johnny !

(PATRICIA *rises.*)

(*Crossing to* R. *of the* COUNT, *wrings his hand.*)   Johnny, you old
sod !   Is it really you ?   Are you all right ?

COUNT.   Yes—please—sank you.

DUSTY (*crossing to* L. *of the* COUNT *and shaking his hand*).
Good show, Count, old cock, old cock !   Good show, sir.

TEDDY (*calling*).   Doris——

PATRICIA (*stopping him quickly*).   Don't !   I'll go and tell her.
It's better.

(*She runs up the stairs.*)

TEDDY (*bringing the* COUNT *down* R.   *Deliriously*).   Johnny, you
wicked old Pole !—What in hell have you been up to ?   Tell us
what happened, Johnny.   Where have you been ?

COUNT.   Please—we fall in se drink.

TEDDY.   Yes, I know you fall in the drink.   How did you get
out of the drink ?   That's what I want to know.

COUNT.   Please—I tell you——

(SWANSON *comes bursting in through the front door, and runs down
between the* COUNT *and* TEDDY.)

SWANSON (*shouting*).   Johnny, you old bastard !   Are you
all right ?   What happened ?   (*To* TEDDY.)   The whole of his

ruddy crew are just piling off a lorry at the guard room—all jabbering like monkeys—and the only thing we can get out of any of them is—" Please we fall in se drink."

TEDDY. That's all we can get out of Johnny up to now.

DUSTY. We haven't given him much of a chance, yet, sir.

TEDDY. Quite right. Quiet, everyone! Come on, Johnny. (*He brings a chair from the table* R., *and sits on it facing the* COUNT.) The floor is yours. You fall in the drink. What happened then ?

COUNT. We—land—pumkek.

TEDDY. Pancake. Yes——

COUNT. We—not hurt—not much. We go pouf——

SWANSON. You go pouf ?

COUNT (*helplessly*). We go pouf.

TEDDY. I've got it. They inflate their rubber dinghy.

COUNT. Dinghy—yes. We—— (*He makes a gesture of rowing. Repeating the gesture.*) No, we—raow—we raow sree hour—see Lysander—far—far—make hola !—No good.

TEDDY. Pilot was having his lunch.

COUNT. We—raow—anosser two hour—sen—get out——

SWANSON. Get out ? Out of the dinghy ? Why ?

COUNT. We walk, please.

SWANSON. You can't ruddy well walk. You're in the ruddy water.

COUNT. Yes, please. We walk in se ruddy water.

DUSTY. They wade ashore, sir.

COUNT. We see—whop.

TEDDY. You see a wop ?

DUSTY. An Eyty ?

COUNT. No, we see—pheasant——

SWANSON. What's a pheasant got to do with it ? You saw a pheasant on the beach ?

COUNT. Not—on—beach. By—gottage.

SWANSON. I still don't see——

TEDDY. He means peasant.

COUNT. Yes, please—peasant in gottage—no telephone. At first—pheasant—peasant—not—understand—'e sink we 'ave parachutes—se enemy—but when 'e see Poland (*he points to the lettering on his arm*) 'e find anosser peasant——

SWANSON. Pheasant.

COUNT. —anosser pheasant wiss big motor. 'E drive us. I see telephone near road. I make to stop and try telephone se aerodrome. I say—please Milchester two-three. Zey say— please, sree hour delay, Winchester. I say—Milchester, please. Zey say—yes, please, Winchester. I say—bloody nuts and we go on.

TEDDY. And here you are, please ?

COUNT. Yes, sank you.

TEDDY. Good old Johnny !

(DORIS *comes down the stairs. There is a pause and the* COUNT *walks across to her and kisses her.*)

DORIS. Hullo, ducky. So you've come back to me.

COUNT (*kisses her hand*). You worry, no ?

DORIS (*smiling*). Oh no. Where have you been ?

COUNT. Please—I fall in ze drink.

DORIS. Yes, I know, but what happened then ?

TEDDY (*imploringly*). Doris—have a heart. He's only just finished telling us the story.

SWANSON. Yes. They all went pouf, and were picked up by pheasants. All sorts of fun and games.

(*They come down to the sofa. The* COUNT *sits on the* R. *arm,* DORIS *on the sofa.*)

DORIS. I'll make him tell me the story later. Only it had better be good, Johnny ducks, after all you've done to me.

(*There is a sudden shiver from* MAUDIE.)

MAUDIE. My 'bus ! I missed it.

DUSTY (*crosses to her*). Cor ! So you 'ave.

SWANSON (*crosses to her*). Doesn't matter, Mrs. Miller. We can't bother about 'buses at a moment like this.

MAUDIE. But I have to bother——

SWANSON. I'll drive you into Lincoln this afternoon.

MAUDIE. That's very kind of you I'm sure, but I'm going to St. Albans.

SWANSON. Or better still, Grantham. Plenty of trains from there.

TEDDY (*crosses to* C., *and stands behind* SWANSON). Don't worry, Mrs. Miller. We'll get you to St. Albans, if we have to fly you there and drop you by parachute.

MAUDIE. I'd rather have gone by 'bus.

TEDDY (*calling*). Percy ! This calls for the party of the century.

(PERCY *enters, sees the* COUNT *and runs to him.*)

PERCY. Cripes, the old Count ! Coo, I'm glad you're back. (*Shaking his hand.*) Where have you been ?

COUNT. Please——

TEDDY
SWANSON } (*together*). He fall in ze drink.

TEDDY. Percy ! Pints for everyone. We'll come and help you. Come on, Dusty. Come on, Gloria.

(SWANSON, TEDDY *and* DUSTY *make for the bar.*)

DUSTY (*going*). I won't be a tick, dear.

MAUDIE. But, Dave, my 'bus !

DUSTY. As far as your 'bus goes, you've had it.

(MAUDIE *goes back to the fire and sits in the armchair below it.* DUSTY *exits into the bar.* DORIS *and the* COUNT *go towards the bar. They stop to kiss.* MRS. OAKES *comes out of her office.*)

MRS. OAKES. Good gracious, the Count ! Well, this is a nice surprise. We'd quite given you up.

(*They shake hands.* MRS. OAKES *goes off carrying her bill book.*)

TEDDY (*coming out*). Gin and lime for you, Doris ?

(PERCY *comes out with two pints, and puts them on the table* R.)

DORIS. Yes, please.

(*They move to the bar.*)

COUNT. Please, I am dirty to go in there.

DORIS. You're filthy to go anywhere, Johnny. But I shouldn't worry just this once.

PERCY. Countess.

(DORIS *stops at the door.*)

What about Bele now ?

DORIS. Bele ? Of course it was Bele. (*She goes to him.*) Thank you ever so much. (*She hugs* PERCY *and cries on his shoulder.*) Silly crying when he's come back.

PERCY. Course not, it's only natural.

DORIS. Well, here he is.

PERCY. No, you keep him.

DORIS. Really ?

PERCY. Never did me any good.

DORIS. Thanks, Percy. I think I will. You never know.

(*They go into the bar.* PETER *appears on the landing and begins to come down the stairs.* DUSTY *and* SWANSON *come from the bar and cross to the fire* L., *each carrying a pint and* DUSTY *has a port for* MAUDIE. PETER *goes to the desk.* MRS. OAKES *appears at the door of the office.*)

MAUDIE. Dave, I don't think I should.

DUSTY. Go on, Maudie. You'll need a few ports if you're going to be dropped by parachute. Won't she, sir ?

SWANSON. Well, Mrs. Miller, here's fluff in your latchkey.

MAUDIE. Fluff in yours !

(TEDDY *runs in from the bar to the foot of the stairs.*)

TEDDY. Pat ! Pat ! Come on down. You don't know what you're missing. Come on, Kyle.

(*He runs back to the bar.* DUSTY *and* SWANSON *are whispering together.*)

MRS. OAKES (*to* KYLE). You'll notice I haven't charged you for the breakfast after all.

PETER. Yes, I see. Thank you very much. (*He pays his bill.*)

MRS. OAKES. By the way, I trust you left the Wing-Commander's things just as they were ?

PETER. Yes, I was very careful.

(PATRICIA *appears on the landing.*)

MRS. OAKES. You could have had Number Two for to-night. I'm sorry you're leaving us so soon.

PETER. I'm afraid (*he turns to the hat-stand and pauses as he sees* PATRICIA) I had no choice. (*He gets his hat off the stand.*)

MRS. OAKES. Good-bye and thank you.

PETER. Thank you.

(MRS. OAKES *goes into the office.*)

PATRICIA (*from the stair*). Good-bye.

PETER. Good-bye, Mrs. Graham.

(*He turns away and exits. There is a burst of laughter from*
DUSTY.)

DUSTY. Go on, sir, tell her the last one—she won't mind.

(SWANSON *whispers to* MAUDIE. *She giggles.* PERCY *enters with another port for* MAUDIE. *Singing is heard in the bar.* PATRICIA *moves to* R. *of the armchair above the fire.*)

PERCY (*crossing to* PATRICIA). Talk about George Formby !
(*Crosses* R.)

MAUDIE (*taking her port*). Tinkety tonk !

SWANSON. Tinkety tonk !

(TEDDY *enters from the bar.*)

TEDDY. We're making old Johnny sing. Come on, Johnny !
(*He crosses to* L. *of* C. *table as* DORIS *enters from the bar, pushing the* COUNT *in front of her.*)

DORIS. Come on, Johnny ! Come on, Fred ! And you, Perc !

(*They make the* COUNT *stand on the* C. *table.*)

COUNT. Oh no, please. I sing so bad.

(*They all gather around and below the table except* PATRICIA *who remains by* L. *armchair.*)

COUNT. (*Sings, helped for the first line by the others*).

> I don't want to join the Air Force,
> I don't want to go to war.
> I'd razzer hang around
> Piccadilly Underground,
> Living on ze earning of a 'igh-born lady . . .

(MRS. OAKES *enters and comes down* R.   JOHNNY *fades on* " 'iqh-
born lady."*)

MRS. OAKES (*severely*).   Quiet, Count !

COUNT (*gets off the table*).   Beg pardon, please.   Sey make me
sing.

TEDDY (*turns to* PATRICIA).   Where's old Kyle ?   Let's make
him join the party.

PATRICIA.   He's gone.

TEDDY.   Gone ?   Oh, pity.   Still, we can do all right without
him.

SWANSON.   Now then, boys and girls !   All together.   Never
mind Mrs. Oakes.   She's heard it before.

> We don't want to join the Air Force,
> We don't want to go to war——

(*They sing in unison.* PATRICIA *stands still, for a moment,
watching.   Then she walks forward to join the group.* TEDDY,
singing lustily, puts an arm around her.)

CURTAIN.

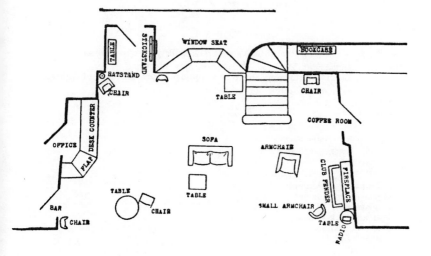

FURNITURE PLOT

1 small settee.	Coal-scuttle.
2 easy chairs.	Fireirons.
5 straight chairs.	Log fire.
1 round table.	Carpets.
2 square tables (same size).	Rugs.
1 occasional table.	Cushions.
1 club fender.	Dressings.
1 hat-stand.	Pictures.
Radio.	Curtains.
Overmantel with mirror.	Letter rack.

4 signs—" Residents only," " Coffee Room," " Lounge Bar," " Private."

Bell-push marked " Waiter " (R. below door).
1 double light switch (R. below door).
1 single light switch (L. below fireplace).

PROPERTY PLOT

ACT I

On Fender.—Tray of tea things : tea-pot, milk jug, cup and saucer.
On Chair Downstage by Fire.—" Everybody's Weekly."
    Bag for DORIS, containing Summer Crop cigarettes, matches or lighter.
On Table by Fire.—Radio.
    Ashtray.
    Magazines.
On C. *Table.*—Ashtray.
On Table R.—Ashtray.
On Table up L.—Flowers.
    Magazines.
    Ashtray.
On Counter.—Telephone.
    Registration forms.
    Registration book.
    Pen and ink-stand.
    Book of rooms.
    Letter rack.
    Handbell.
    Time table.
    Phone books.
    Bill book.
    Tray.
    Ashtray.
Window open, curtains open, doors shut.

Off Stage up R.—Cigarettes in case, matches, suitcase, money (coins and
    paper money), hat and coat (PETER KYLE).
    Small suitcase, umbrella, gas-mask (MAUDIE).
    Telegram (MRS. OAKES).
Off Stage down R.—3 tin trays.
    1 gin and lime, pink gin, pint of beer (*1st Entrance.*)
    Gin and lime, pink gin, 3 pints of beer (*2nd Entrance*).
    Pink gin (*3rd Entrance*).
    2 pink gins, 1 gin and lime (*4th Entrance*).
    3 pints of beer (*5th Entrance*).
    1 pink gin, pint of beer (*6th Entrance*).

ACT II, SCENE 1

Off Stage R.—Set of darts.
    Glass of gin and ginger (DORIS).
    Rug (SWANSON).
    Written note (" Suggested that Flight-Lieutenant Graham, etc ").
Off Stage L.—Ring (PATRICIA).
On Table R.—Tray with coffee-pot, milk-jug, sugar basin, cup and saucer,
    spoon.
On Counter.—Bag (DORIS).
On Fender.—Newspaper and magazine.
    Cup of coffee.

82

On L. *Arm of Sofa.*—Box of matches.
Logs in coal-scuttle.
Curtains shut, doors shut.

ACT II, SCENE 2

Off Stage L.—1 tray with 5 knives, 5 forks, 5 large plates, 2 servers (spoon
  and fork), cruet, marmalade jar, butter dish, toast rack, 5 cups and
  saucers.
  2nd tray with 2 entrée dishes (with bacon and eggs), milk and coffee
  jugs.
  Handkerchief, cigarette case (PATRICIA).
Off Stage R.—Flask, bloodstained handkerchief (TEDDY).
Centre curtains open.

ACT III

On Chair above Fire.—Bag (DORIS), containing cigarettes, matches, letter
  from JOHNNY.
  Magazine.
On Table C.—Tray of coffee for one.
Off Stage R.—Tray with 5 clean ashtrays.
  Tray with brandy and small bottle of soda.
  1 pint of beer.
  2 ports.
  1 gin-and-lime.
  5 pints of beer.
  Bele, duster (PERCY).
  Small parcel containing cotton wool, bandage, iodine (PATRICIA).
  5 pieces of paper, coins and paper money (PETER KYLE).
Off Stage L.—Suitcase (PETER KYLE).
  Bandage and pin (TEDDY).
  Gas-mask, umbrella, small suitcase (MAUDIE).
  Pile of linen (MRS. OAKES).

Curtains open, doors shut.

EFFECTS PLOT

1 double turntable panatrope.
2 speakers.
1 bass drum.

ACT I

Cue 1.—B.B.C. music—to fade as MRS. OAKES enters.

Cue 2.—Car door slam. (During music.)

Cue 3.—Car driving away. (During music and to fade as PETER enters.)

Cue 4.—B.B.C. Announcer, after slight pause on:
          MRS. OAKES. " I'm sorry."

Cue 5.—Fade in bombers at a distance on:
          DORIS. " Will you have a cigarette, Mr. Kyle ? "

Cue 6.—Bring in bombers overhead on:
          DORIS. " Tell me, do you know Carmen Miranda
          or Bing Crosby ? "
—then fade, during next speech.

Cue 7.—Damaged bomber overhead. Fade in quickly on:
          DORIS. " Fancy ! Whatever's he like ? "

Cue 8.—Damaged bomber landing, on:
          DORIS. " There's something wrong with that one."

Cue 9.—Quick fade-out of bomber on:
          PETER. " My God, so it is. It's coming in."

Cue 10.—Damaged bomber taxi-ing back on:
          PETER. " I think so. It's gone out of sight behind
          those hangars."

Cue 11.—Fade out taxi-ing on:
          DORIS. " . . . the famous Chinese pilot—Wun
          Wing Low."

Cue 12.—Car door slam, after TEDDY exits, end of act, as DORIS passes
PATRICIA and touches her arm.

Cue 13.—Car driving away (almost immediately after *Cue* 12) as MRS.
OAKES crosses to window to draw curtains. Fade out as CURTAIN
falls.

ACT II, SCENE 1

Cue 1.—B.B.C. Announcer. To cut off on:
          PATRICIA. " Turn it off."

Cue 2.—German bomber in the distance. Fade in on:
          MAUDIE. " Tinkety-tonk." (*Exit* DORIS.)

Cue 3.—Distant gunfire on:
          MAUDIE. " Perhaps you don't listen for it like
          what I do."
—followed by quick fade-out of German bomber.

Cue 4.—Take-off. (*A*) Fade in with gradual crescendo and fade-out on:
          SWANSON. " There's one off, thank God."
          (*B*) Fade in again on:
          SWANSON. " Worse than landing."
          (*C*) Quick fade-in loud and fade-out on:
          SWANSON. " He must have cleared that by inches."

Cue 5.—Machine-gun fire and four bomb explosions on:

SWANSON ⎱ *(together).* ⎰ " God ! "
PATRICIA ⎰ ⎱ " Why have they turned
out the flare path ? "

Cue 6.—Repeat Machine-guns. Then heavy, sharp explosion, and tearing sound of aircraft destroyed on:

SWANSON. " Brakes, you idiot ! Brakes ! Don't take off ! "

ACT II, SCENE 2

Cue 1.—Bomber landing and taxi-ing back as CURTAIN rises.

Cue 2.—Fade-out taxi-ing on:

PATRICIA. " I must have been asleep. Are either of them Teddy's ? "

Cue 3.—Car pulling up . . . door slam . . . drives away on:

PATRICIA. " I wish I understood. You're very brave."

ACT III

No effects.

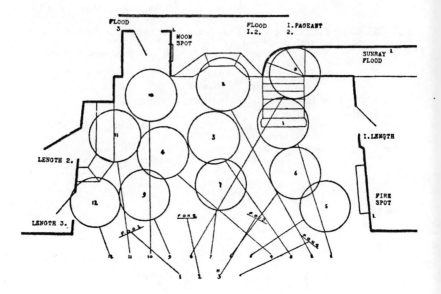

LIGHTING PLOT

No. 1 Batten.—3 circuits—51, 7, 3.
No. 4 Batten.—4 circuits—2, white, 4, 16.
Floats.—4 circuits—51, 7, 3, 4.
3 *Lengths.*—Mixed amber and white.
3 *Floods.*—3 No. 3 mediums.
2 *Pageants.*
4 *Wall Fittings.*—4 No. 15 bulbs.
Fire.
Fire Spot.—Mixed red and amber medium.
Focus Spot.—No. 17 blue.
Sunray.—No. 3.
12 *Spots.*—1, 2, 3, 4, 5, 9, 11—51
    7, 8, 10, 12—3.
    6—7.
4 *F.O.H.*—1, 2, 3—51.
    4—7

ACT 1

To Open.—Pageants—2 FULL.
    Floods (3)—3 FULL.
    Fire—on.
    Sunray on stairs (3)—on.
    3 door lengths—on.

Spots.—12—all FULL.
  4 F.O.H.—all FULL.
No. 1 *Batten.*—Pink at 12.
  Straw at 12.
No. 4 *Batten.*—Amber at FULL.
  2 white circuits FULL.
Floats.—Gold at 8.
  Pink at 12.
  Straw at 12.
1st Cue.—Fade is 10 *minutes.*
  No. 1 Batten and floats. No. 6 Spot and pageants to—15.

ACT II, SCENE 1

To Open.—Fire on.
  Fire spot on.
  3 lengths on.
  Moonlight spot on.
  Sunray on.
No. 1 *Batten.*—Pink at FULL.
No. 4 *Batten.*—Blue at 13.
Floats.—Pink at 8.
  Straw at 15.
  Gold at 15.
Spots.—2 and 6 at 10.
  The rest FULL.
  4 F.O.H. FULL.
  R. and L. fittings on.
Cue 1.—Snap B.O., leaving—fire, L. sunray, No. 4 *Batten.*
Cue 2.—Snap in—R. fittings.
  Floats—pink 8, straw 12, gold 15.
Cue 3.—B.O. as *Cue* 1.
Cue 4.—Snap in—Floats—pink at 8.
  L. fittings.
  Spots 1, 3, 5, 6, 7, FULL.
  F.O.H. 1, 2, 3, FULL.
Cue 5.—B.O. as *Cue* 1.
Cue 6.—Snap in—Floats—pink 8, straw 15, gold 15.
  R. fittings.
  Spots 1, 3, 7, 9, 10, 11, 12, to FULL.
  F.O.H. 1, 2, 3, 4, to FULL.

ACT II, SCENE 2

To Open.—Floats—amber at 20.
  No. 4 Batten—blue at 15.
  Fire on.
Cue 1.—Snap in lighting as Act II, Scene 1, *Cue* 6.
Cue 2.—Fade in No. 4 Batten—2 white circuits FULL, amber circuit FULL.
Cue 3.—Fade on wheel—No. 1 Batten out.
  Floats—pink and straw out.
  Spots—6 and 5 out.

ACT III

To Open.—2 pageants FULL.
   3 floods (white) FULL.
   Sunray on.
   3 lengths on.

No. 1 Batten.—Gold at 7.
   Straw at 7.
   Pink at 7.

Floats.—Gold at 7.
   Pink at 7.
   Straw at 7.

No. 4 Batten.—2 white circuits FULL.
   Amber circuit FULL.

Spots.—All FULL.
   4 F.O.H. FULL.